T0399340

Drama for the Inclusive Classroom

Incorporate drama and improvisation into your classroom to build confidence, support social-emotional learning, and engage every student in the curriculum. This book's detailed and easy-to-implement chapters walk you through using drama to develop critical listening and communication skills, conflict resolution abilities, behavior regulation, and even grow new skills in math, literature, geography, and more! Each chapter builds on the skills learned in previous lessons, allowing you to increase the complexity as students progress. Designed for use with inclusive classrooms as well as dedicated special education programs, this guide features adaptable activities to include students at every ability level.

Sally Bailey is Professor of Theatre and Director of the Drama Therapy Program at Kansas State University, USA. She also directs the Barrier-Free Theatre for adults with and without disabilities for the Manhattan Parks and Recreation Department.

Other Eye on Education Books
Available From Routledge (www.routledge.com/k-12)

**Sexuality for All Abilities: Teaching and Discussing
Sexual Health in Special Education**
Katie Thune and Molly Gage

**Coding as a Playground: Programming and Computational Thinking in the Early
Childhood Classroom, Second Edition**
Marina Umaschi Bers

Culturally Responsive Self-Care Practices for Early Childhood Educators
Julie Nicholson, Priya Shimpi Driscoll, Julie Kurtz, Doménica Márquez, and
LaWanda Wesley

**Implementing Project Based Learning in Early Childhood: Overcoming
Misconceptions and Reaching Success**
Sara Lev, Amanda Clark, and Erin Starkey

**Advocacy for Early Childhood Educators: Speaking Up for Your Students,
Your Colleagues, and Yourself**
Colleen Schmit

**Grit, Resilience, and Motivation in Early Childhood: Practical Takeaways
for Teachers**
Lisa B. Fiore

Drama for the Inclusive Classroom

Activities to Support Curriculum and Social-Emotional Learning

Sally Bailey

Routledge
Taylor & Francis Group

NEW YORK AND LONDON

First published 2021
by Routledge
52 Vanderbilt Avenue, New York, NY 10017

and by Routledge
2 Park Square, Milton Park, Abingdon, Oxon, OX14 4RN

Routledge is an imprint of the Taylor & Francis Group, an informa business

Library of Congress Cataloging-in-Publication Data
Names: Bailey, Sally D., author.
Title: Drama for the inclusive classroom : activities to support curriculum and social-emotional learning / Sally Bailey.
Description: New York, NY : Routledge, 2021. | Series: Other eye on education | Includes bibliographical references.
Identifiers: LCCN 2021001269 (print) | LCCN 2021001270 (ebook) | ISBN 9780367859473 (hardback) | ISBN 9780367860042 (paperback) | ISBN 9781003016373 (ebook)
Subjects: LCSH: Inclusive education–Curricula. | Drama–Therapeutic use. | Drama in education. | Affective education.
Classification: LCC LC1200 .B35 2021 (print) | LCC LC1200 (ebook) | DDC 371.39/9–dc23
LC record available at https://lccn.loc.gov/2021001269
LC ebook record available at https://lccn.loc.gov/2021001270

ISBN: 978-0-367-85947-3 (hbk)
ISBN: 978-0-367-86004-2 (pbk)
ISBN: 978-1-003-01637-3 (ebk)

Typeset in Optima
by KnowledgeWorks Global Ltd.

Contents

About the Author

Sally Bailey, MFA, MSW, RDT/BCT believes that the arts and creative expression are natural inborn abilities of all people and that everyone should have the opportunity to experience them and express themselves. She is a Registered Drama Therapist and Board Certified Trainer for Drama Therapy. She worked with recovering substance abusers and people with disabilities of all ages in the Washington, DC area for over ten years.

Currently, Sally is a Professor of Theatre, the Director of the Drama Therapy Program, and a member of the Gerontology faculty at Kansas State University in Manhattan, Kansas. She directs the Barrier-Free Theatre, a theatre troupe of adults with and without disabilities. Her book *Barrier-Free Theatre: Including Everyone in Theatre Arts – in Schools, Recreation, and Arts Programs – Regardless of (Dis)Ability* was the recipient of the American Alliance for Theatre in Education's 2011 Distinguished Book Award.

A past president of the North American Drama Therapy Association (NADTA), she received NADTA's Gertrud Schattner Award for distinguished contribution to the field of drama therapy in education, publication, practice, and service and the 2018 NADTA award for Teaching Excellence. In 2007, she was given the Distinguished Service Award in Arts and Disabilities, recognizing outstanding support for the arts and children with disabilities presented by Accessible Arts, Kansas City, KS and the Kansas State Board of Education.

For more information on accessible theatre, drama for people with disabilities, and drama therapy in general, visit her website: www.dramatherapycentral.com

Introduction

The purpose of this book is to de-mystify how to begin using drama in special education and inclusive classrooms in manageable chunks so teachers and school counselors can build their skills and self-confidence along with their students. This introduction provides general guidelines in terms of what teachers and counselors should expect as they begin to do drama games and activities with students who have not experienced drama before. Finally, the introduction explains how each chapter will progress and what will be covered in each.

Many teachers intuit that drama is motivating and interesting to students and that it could be helpful for delivering curricular content as well as for improving social-emotional skills. They are absolutely correct; however, incorporating drama into their classroom can feel intimidating, because most teachers have not had training in educational drama. The same goes for school counselors who have not had training in educational drama or drama therapy. If either of these descriptions sound familiar, this book is for you!

Drama activities typically do not happen at a desk. They require an open space in which students can move about. Because many special education and some late-maturing neurotypical students lack the ability to manage their own bodies in space, behavior problems can appear when they get up from their desks. Desks serve as a type of behavior management device because they create a safe, personal space for each student with clear physical boundaries. While sitting in their seats, students are not going to bump into other students. However, once out of their chairs, those boundaries disappear, and students can start colliding. Being distracted by the need to manage classroom traffic or behavior challenges pulls a teacher away from focusing on involving the students in drama. In these unfortunate cases, an unpleasant time is had by all.

Creating plays has been shown to have many educational and social-emotional benefits for students, but play production is an advanced form of drama. In addition, rehearsing and performing a play requires social skills and executive functions some students may not have developed yet. The result can be chaos. Using an already scripted play is too advanced for many young students because memorization of lines becomes a barrier to dramatic expression. What drama educators learn during their training is that in the beginning levels of educational drama, *the play* is not the thing; instead *playing* (or improvising) carefully targeted drama games and activities is the appropriate place to start.

The purpose of this book is to de-mystify how to begin using drama in special education and inclusive classrooms in manageable chunks so teachers and counselors can build their skills and self-confidence along with their students. Short, discrete drama interventions can highlight the strengths that students have and address deficits they need to work on. Specifically, many drama games and improvisation exercises build executive functioning skills, such as attenuation, attention switching, sequencing, initiation, inhibition, task planning, task organization, self-reflection, and even working memory. This book can be your handbook for developing the necessary skills to guide students in group activities. Early dramatic experiences can scaffold more advanced techniques and sequentially pilot students from simpler levels of executive functions and social-emotional learning skills to more complex ones.

Time devoted to drama in the classroom is never wasted. It provides students with brain and body breaks. They can get up from their desks, practice emotional and behavioral regulation, and release tension in a positive way. Once students can work together and regulate their behavior, teachers can employ drama to explore parts of the curriculum, making lessons more memorable. Students will become motivated to learn as lessons become more active and concrete. The enjoyment of drama will transfer to all aspects of learning!

Layout of the Book and What to Expect

Chapter One addresses the basic skills that teachers and school counselors need in order to lead a drama group. The structure for a drama lesson – Warm-up, Activity, De-roling, Discussion, and Closure – is explained. The importance of inclusive learning and respect is described as well as positive ways of getting past differences that might keep students from working together. This is useful whether working in an inclusive class of students who are neurotypical and neurodiverse, in a special education class with students who have a wide variety of needs, or when two separate classrooms decide to share drama time together.

As humans we have a tendency to see ourselves as members of different teams: "us" and "them," instead of as "us." Some basic guidelines for making accommodations and adaptions are included so opportunities can be created for everyone to participate on a level playing field. Finally, the solid pedagogical reasons for using drama as a teaching tool are provided in case you have to convince administrators or fellow teachers that including drama in your classroom will create positive outcomes in academics as well as in learning social-emotional skills.

Chapter Two: Developing Executive Functions through Drama explains the various aspects of executive functions: The cognitive skills that are necessary for students to organize their thoughts and focus their emotions and behaviors on the tasks of learning and living successfully. While most drama games and activities address more than one executive function at the same time, they will be presented in groupings under specific executive functions that they seem to most strongly address. For example, the game Change Three helps students develop working memory, attention skills, and observation skills, but it is especially strong at developing working memory. When activities are organized in this manner, you, the teacher or counselor, will begin to recognize other games and activities not in this book that could be added to your arsenal for helping students grow the specific executive functions they need.

Chapter Three: Building on Thinking and Social-Emotional Skills through Drama provides drama games that are more advanced. They focus on executive functions and complex skills, such as listening, communication, and working as a cooperative team. Students will most likely continue to enjoy the games in Chapter Two. However, when they are ready to move on to more complex work, they will also enjoy the challenge of the Chapter Three games. Even if you think your students have basic executive functioning skills, starting with Chapter Three games may be too advanced for students not used to the behavior regulation required when drama is incorporated into the classroom.

Chapter Four introduces improvisation and role play. Improvisation is not just a skill for creating free-form comedy. It has grown and diversified through the years as it has been applied to education, therapy, business and corporate relations, medical training, scientific communication, and conflict resolution. There are a few important skills that improvisers (and those side coaching them) need to know to achieve success and avoid anarchy. This chapter will put you on the right path.

Chapter Five rounds out the use of drama in the classroom by providing ideas of how to integrate drama seamlessly into teaching the academic subjects in your curriculum. As you will have experienced by the time you get to this chapter, embodied learning is not only motivating and engaging for students, it sticks with them longer than information learned via lecture, video, or paper and pencil only.

Games and improvisations have not been divided by grade. These activities can be played by all ages from first grade through adulthood. If you are teaching first or second grade, you may decide that the games in Chapter Three require a bit more attention and inhibition skills than your students are ready for. If so, stick with the games in Chapter Two. Each class is going to be unique because of the level of executive functioning of the students in it. I have played many of these games with people from six to eighty-six, and every single one of them has enjoyed themselves.

My hope is that for teachers this book helps you courageously branch out and become a more effective group leader and teacher: Flexible, creative, and ready to take on any challenge that comes up in your classroom. For school counselors, my hope is that you find new ways to guide students through their confusion and hurt through connecting positively to others and finding value in themselves. I would love feedback on how your experiences have gone: What has been successful and what needs to be explained more clearly.

My philosophy of education is first: Learning should be fun! So, enjoy!

The Basics of Leading Drama in the Classroom

Basic Skills Students Need for Participating in Drama

Before using drama as a tool for social-emotional learning or teaching curricular material, teachers and counselors need to start from where the students are in terms of group abilities and expectations. Drama activities typically do not happen at a desk. Students need to be out of their chairs either in an open space, sitting in a circle, or working in small groups, perhaps around a table or several desks pushed together.

There will be some noise involved, because students need to communicate verbally with each other, and sometimes the volume may rise when they get excited, or if they get frustrated and need to work out differences of opinion. Noise and movement does not necessarily mean students are out of control; often they indicate students are deeply engaged and excited. There is a clear difference in the quality of the sound in a classroom that appears on the surface to be chaotic and one that is actually in chaos. Students in control of the creative process are focused on the activity; students who are unfocused and not on task are fooling around or showing off.

Drama requires self-discipline and self-control. To learn how to remain in control, especially at the beginning, students need careful scaffolding. Directions for how to play the activities suggested in this book will be included with each description as well as Helpful Hints to simplify, clarify, or vary it.

If you have students who have difficulty staying focused whenever they leave their seats, then start with games that help students develop their executive functions. Take your time and repeat games they like often to provide practice with those skills.

Students should think of drama as an enjoyable part of their school day, but not as indoor recess. Accordingly, think through what you want to call the dramatic activities you are going to be doing. Theatre professionals call the activities you will find in this book "drama games." Sheldon Patinkin (2000), one of the founders of Second City in Chicago, says:

> The improvisational games aren't games in the sense of winning and losing, and they aren't about being funny. They are about being in the moment; they are about being totally present to each other onstage – being "in play." (p. 22)

Notice, he says "in play," not "in a play" or "playing around."

If the word "game" sends the wrong message to your students, avoid that term. You may find:

- Self-expression
- Drama
- Creative drama
- Practicing the ability to _____[insert name of skill]
- Explorations
- Challenges or
- Experiments

work better for your class. You could say something like:

> We are going to do an experiment about focusing today. You will be challenged to use your concentration abilities during this experiment. When we are done, I want you to tell me on a scale of one to ten [or one to five] how well you were able to concentrate.

I will alternate between the terms drama, activity, game, experiment, exploration, and challenge throughout the book to provide variety for you as reader.

One way to help students develop self-control is to emphasize their responsibility in making the experiment a success. They need to bring self-control to the experiment you are going to do together as a group.

The more self-control they display during an activity, and the more they follow your directions, the more they will learn and the more fun they will have.

If they cannot bring their self-control (or focus or self-discipline or whatever developmentally appropriate term you want to use) to the experiment, the whole class will not be successful, and everyone will have to sit down. The consequence of stopping drama early does not need to be worded as a threat, a warning, or a punishment; it can be delivered in terms of enlisting each individual student's commitment:

> I need each one of you to follow directions and pay attention to your body's movements in space. As long as you are listening and being careful, you won't get hurt and neither will anyone else.

If you have students who like to police others' behavior, you can also add:

> Everyone is being responsible for themselves; there is no need to pay attention to anyone else's behavior.

Another approach can put the focus on creating group safety:

> As long as everyone is safe, we can do these experiments, but if you put yourself or someone else in harm's way, you will have to sit out.

Having students sit out is best accomplished if there is a para-professional or assistant who can engage those taken out of the activity in something else productive or take them aside to talk about why they could not follow directions.

The best way to keep a group engaged and behaving positively is usually not to remove anyone, but to keep them all participating. Often the most distractive behavior comes from players who are "out" and have nothing to do. When someone is bored, it becomes very easy for them to "make excitement" by teasing or bothering someone else who is also "out." Most of the drama activities in this book will not involve elimination or "outs" for that reason. One way to keep everyone participating is by using games that do not eliminate players. I call these "Odd-Person-In" games. Elephant and Giraffe and 1776 are two of the Odd-Person-In games in the book.

Competitive activities can be problematic in a classroom, especially when students are trying to develop self-control. Yes, the adult world is filled with competition, but before students can begin to handle losing and winning, they first need to improve their abilities to work cooperatively. Competition creates a deficit-based situation for whichever team loses, resulting in unhappy feelings. It makes more sense to create a strengths-based space and generate feelings of safety among students. This book focuses on learning how to participate within a group cooperatively, not on how to win.

Developing Belief in Yourself as a Teacher or Counselor Using Drama

Just as students will be starting from where they are in terms of drama, teachers and counselors will be starting from where *they* are. Many educators feel intimidated about incorporating drama into their classroom or therapy room, because they do not have formal drama training. I guarantee that if you have the skills to run a classroom or a therapy group, you have the skills to facilitate the drama activities in this book. If group facilitation skills were not focused on in your training, you can learn them.

Part of leading group activities involves establishing group norms, creating clear structure, and providing simple instructions. I will go over these with each activity and offer examples of proactive ways to give directions. Of course, you will want to translate them into your own words.

In terms of drama training, whether you know it or not, you actually already have had a lot of experience in drama. While you may not have ever been in a play or taken a theatre class, between the ages of one-and-a-half and two you began naturally to participate in imitation and dramatic play. This is an instinctive activity that children initiate in the preoperational stage of child development (Flavell, 1963; Piaget, 1962). Until the age of five or six, you continued to learn in large part through acting out people and situations, sometimes by yourself and sometimes with your friends and family. Because of these experiences, you are a drama expert. Even if you last played dramatically thirty years ago, you will find that doing drama is like riding a bicycle: Once you start again, the ability quickly comes back to you.

Child psychologist Lev Vygotsky (1978, 1986) believed that children learn about the social world by enacting it and through that process develop their social skills. As they solve problems while acting out scenes, they begin to understand the world around them better. Often children who do not have adults to scaffold these dramatic play skills for them or who lack other children to play with are in need of these skills. The lack of these skills negatively affects the ability to function appropriately in a classroom and in other social settings. If you experience difficulties when you start doing drama activities with your students, lack of enough early dramatic play may be a reason. You may have to practice the basic skills in Chapter Two longer. That's fine. Moving on to more advanced drama activities is not required, and your class is not on a timetable. Practice the basics until students have mastered them.

A big part of successfully leading a drama group is presenting yourself to your students with confidence. Undoubtedly, you are able to do this when you are teaching your academic specialty. Transfer this confidence to drama. Imagine yourself in your most self-assured, empowered, and relaxed state, when you are presenting your favorite lesson plan or doing an activity you truly enjoy. Can you remember what it feels like to be doing this? What words and images come to your mind? Write down those words and images so you can remember them. Before you teach each drama lesson, take a moment to bring those feelings and images back to your heart and mind. This kind of preparation is an acting technique created by the famous Russian acting teacher Constantin Stanislavski (1948) called "sense memory." The actor transfers an emotional experience from a remembered event to a moment on stage currently being performed. Sense memory is easier to do with positive experiences than difficult ones.

Drama leaders typically are meant to play many of the games in the book with the students, serving as a role model. Your participation helps the game to function smoothly. Other times it is more important to be outside the game watching and coaching. The instructions for each game will indicate whether you are a coach, a participant, or serve a different function.

The drama activities in Chapter Two focus on helping students develop basic executive functions and self-regulation skills so that they can successfully perform in the freedom of a drama setting. These skills are also needed for learning and handling oneself in all work and social areas in life. Later, after students develop these basic skills, Chapters Three, Four, and Five will introduce more complex activities, involving advanced problem solving, social interaction, and teamwork.

The Basics of Teaching a Drama Game/Experiment

There are a few basics involved in teaching any drama game or activity. As we get older and become more experienced, we often forget how complex many of the tasks are that we do every day. As an adult, we do not need to think about the activity while doing it, because it has become part of our procedural memory and is now automatic. Some of the instructions in this section may seem to be presented in an extremely obvious, simplistic, and detailed manner. I am consciously reverse engineering all the steps in a described process so anyone doing the task with a group for the first time will know exactly what sequences are involved.

How to Plan a Session

A drama session typically moves from a short *warm-up game* that engages everyone, followed by a *main activity* or two or three (depending on the complexity of the activity and the general time it takes to play it), followed by *discussion* and *de-roling,* and ends with a short *closure.* Plan to alternate all drama activities from passive to active to passive or from active to passive to active. If you use this alternating structure, students will not become too wound up from the active parts and will have a chance to catch their breath during the passive parts. An active-active-active session could either have students bouncing off the ceiling because they are so wired or ready to fall sleep because they have been exhausted. A passive-passive-passive session may have students getting bored and acting out or ready to fall asleep.

Think through the skills you want your students to learn. Providing practice for a variety of skills in one session may be more engaging for students than practicing the same skill with all of your activities. A good design would be to choose games that have different structures and goals. For instance, if you play an "odd person in" game in which students are exchanging places, follow that with a passing game, a guessing game, or a story creation game. Vary students' physical game positions between sitting, standing, and moving. Closures almost always should be passive and thoughtful.

Preparation

Before teaching any game/experiment, the space needs to be prepared. If your classroom is filled with desks and chairs, guide your students to adjust the space. Some activities require an open area in which students can create a circle of chairs. Sometimes an activity needs open space to move around in. Sometimes a separate performing space and audience space need to be set up. The instructions for each game will identify what type of space requirements are needed.

Think of the simplest way to break down the steps of rearranging your room. Give students one direction at a time. For instance:

> Everyone stand up at your desk. [Pause.]
>
> Pick up your desk. Now move it to the back of the room. Take your time; you don't have to rush. [Pause.]
>
> When you get there, stand by your desk. [Pause.]
>
> Now go back to your chair. [Pause]
>
> Pick up your chair and move it to create a large circle in the room. [Pause.]
>
> Stand by your chair. [Pause.]
>
> Good. I think we need the circle to be a little bit bigger. Please, move your chair back about a foot. [Pause.]
>
> Now, everyone, sit in your chair.

Always have students stand or sit in the configuration in which the game will be played before starting to give directions for it. Less working memory is required when you do this. They will not have to imagine where they *will* be as you describe how to play the game; they are already there.

As you explain each part of the game, demonstrate it and have students practice it with you so they can feel it in their bodies. Everyone will understand the game better, especially anyone who has difficulty with attention, sequencing, auditory processing, or sensory integration. In addition to saying "left" and "right," also use gestures to show which side you mean.

Do at least one practice round. Stop. Ask if that made sense to everyone. Practicing a round allows students the chance to ask questions and rehearse sequences before their actions officially "count" in the game. If you need a second practice round, that's fine.

Warm-up

Most of the games in Chapters Two and Three are warm-up games. Warm-ups help students let go of past thoughts, focus their minds and bodies in the here-and-now, connect with the other people in the group, and engage their enthusiasm. In the beginning of incorporating drama in your classroom, plan your session around these warm-up games because they teach executive functions and basic teamwork. When students are ready to move on to more advanced activities using improvisation and role-play in Chapters Four and Five, refer back to Chapters Two and Three for a warm-up to start your session. This helps focus and engage students. Once everyone is on the same page, it is easier to listen and work together.

When to End a Game

It is important to be aware of the group's engagement or lack thereof while playing a game, so the leader knows when to bring it to an end. When students are totally engaged, their energy is high, and their attention is strong. As they continue to play, you will sense the engagement building. When you sense that students are almost at their most intense enjoyment of the game is the time to prepare for bringing the game to an end. You will be able to feel the moment coming; it feels similar to the energy experienced when a roller coaster car is almost at the top of a hill, right before it crests.

Give students a warning that "There are three rounds left," or "We'll take two more turns and then we'll stop." Then stick to your warning, even if they moan and groan, and move into a discussion or onto a new game. Ending before the players are bored or have mastered a game means they will want to play it again and will continue to find it intriguing. If you wait too long to end the game – after their engagement has peaked and the excitement is waning – you have waited too long. If that happens, stop immediately and move on to something else.

Warning students that the end of a game is coming is much better than stopping it abruptly. They feel cheated if they don't have time to prepare for the end. This is particularly helpful for students who have difficulty with inhibiting behavior and making transitions.

If you sense students are ready to quit a game very soon after they have started that probably means that the game was too simple for them. Stop and see if you can add a level of difficulty to it. I literally say, "OK, that was level one. NOW we're going to learn level two!" If that does not re-engage them, then stop, and move onto another game. You can try the more complicated version another time, if you want.

On the other hand, students could be ready to quit a game because it is too difficult for them. That will become readily apparent when too many mistakes are being made. Double check to make sure they understand the rules. If they don't, re-explain using more examples, and if you see "the light bulb" go off over their heads, you will know you can continue. If not, you may need to either take away a complication of the game to make it simpler or just move on to something else.

Discussion and De-roling

At the end of an intensive game or improvisation, it is important to take a few minutes for discussion and de-roling. Drama experiments generate lots of ideas and many discussion points. One of the keys to getting a good discussion going is to start with open-ended questions about the students' experiences with the experiment (What was that like? How did that feel?), move to close-ended questions to get more details (Did you get dizzy doing that spin? Did you prefer being a follower or a leader?), and then return to open-ended questions (Did that experiment remind you of anything in your life? How could you use that idea when you are doing math?)

An important aspect of discussions, which most people forget about, is the importance of wait-time. Often not enough time is allowed for students to think of a comment or an answer because the teacher feels uncomfortable waiting in the silence. Reflective answers about experiences take longer to formulate than answers about facts. Students need to evaluate what they felt physically, emotionally, and cognitively and put words to those experiences. They will need even longer to formulate a question of their own. That requires searching for what they know and what they do not understand, figuring out how to frame the question to get the answer they need, and then finding words to fit into that frame.

Typically, teachers wait from 0.07 to 2 seconds before they expect an answer to a question. That is not enough time for students to process most questions, come up with an answer, and raise their hand, even if it is a simple answer to a close-ended question. Students need longer "wait-time" (Rowe, 1986) or "think-time" (Stahl, 1994). Give them a pause of between five and ten (or more) seconds. It is useful to allow additional think time after a student responds, so other students can take it in and come up with a response of their own. This is how great discussions get started. (Think-time is often a better term to use for this need because typically in our US culture the word waiting connotes wasting time. Giving students time to think is never a waste!)

The first time you use think-time will seem interminable, but you will get used to it! It can be helpful to say directly, "I am going to wait for five to ten seconds to give you a chance to think about your answer," so students do not become intimidated by the silence. To keep the mood light, I will sometimes hum the Jeopardy Question Song until someone puts up their hand.

Think-time is especially helpful for a class that includes students with disabilities and neurotypical students. Generally, students who have cognitive disabilities need more processing time. They will be able to come up with their own original ideas and reactions if enough time is given for their receptive (intake) and expressive (output) processes to be completed.

If students recognize an activity that helped them with some aspect of thinking, feeling, or behaving with which they have been struggling, ask if they want to be reminded of that new skill later when they need it in class. Is there a code word or clue they would like to be used to remind them if you see them struggling? For instance, if Phil has discovered that closing his eyes for a moment and taking a deep breath helps him re-focus and pay attention to his math problems when he starts to feel distracted, you might say, "Deep breath" as a reminder. If he would prefer a word that does not sound like an order coming from the teacher, the word or phrase could be an animal or machine that takes deep breaths like "Opera Singer," "Whale," or "Bellows." In this way, the lessons that are learned through drama experiments can be employed in other learning or social situations.

There will be days when the activities do not generate a lot of discussion. This may be due to the game itself, the mood of the group, the weather outside, or the environment you are working in. Everything does not need to end in a long discussion. My guess is that students will continue thinking about the experiments and talk about them later.

If a game or improvisation has brought up a lot of excitement or a strong emotion, it will be important to *de-role* students. *De-roling* is the process of releasing emotions and leaving the character or situation of a game or improvisation behind. De-roling can be as simple as quickly shaking out the body and taking a slow deep breath to come back to oneself. This resets the muscles of the body which have taken on the tension of the particular emotion or character. A few moments for some deep breathing can also help de-role students. You can support the de-roling process by saying "Breathe out the character (or emotion) and breathe in yourself at peace (or relaxation)."

Another way to de-role: Ask students to pretend they are within the body and costume of their character. Tell them to unzip the whole character from the top of their head to their toes. Take the character or emotion off like it is a costume and throw it into the middle of the circle.

Another dramatic means of de-roling is to have a prop – maybe a pool noodle – and pretend you are "spraying" the character or emotion off the students. If this would end up being more distracting for certain students and not create the sense of closure you need, use a different de-roling method.

A "de-roling machine," similar to a "car wash," can also "wash the role (or emotions) away." Students make two lines facing each other and assist in the de-roling process by pretending to soap, clean, rinse, and dry each student as they go through the "de-roling machine." The machine parts do not touch the actors; however, sounds and movements can be made! Typically, the student at the "top left" of the "entrance" to the "de-roling machine" enters first, followed by the student at the "top right." As they move through the "de-roling machine," they imagine the character and emotions are being pleasantly and thoroughly washed off them. When they reach the end, they re-join the line on the side from which they started. This way – like a conveyor belt – each student can go through the "de-roling machine" and come out rejuvenated!

Closure

When your drama explorations are completed, take a few moments for closure to calm students and transition them from the excitement of being actively up on their feet to downshift to a quieter academic setting.

A closure can be a short discussion about what was just completed: What students experienced physically, emotionally, and/or cognitively, and how they can relate it to other aspects of school or life. It could be a go-around in a circle with each student saying one word or phrase about what they learned today or "took away" from their exploration. The final part of closure would be to calmly return any desks and chairs that had been moved back to their original places.

Clear Class Guidelines

In recent years, civility seems to have left public discourse and being rude is in fashion. On TV and social media, students see adults insult and mock each other in a manner that is very un-adult. The best way to circumvent students participating in put-downs and micro-aggressions is to begin your first drama session with talking about Guidelines for Respect. The most buy-in for these guidelines will occur if students are involved in their creation. That does not mean that you as the teacher do not have veto power or that you cannot add your own guidelines into the mix.

Formulate the class code of conduct as much as you can in terms of "thou shalts" as opposed to "thou shalt nots." Stating the behavior that is expected as the norm is more effective than saying what not to do. A good way to frame your guideline creation is to say:

> We want these guidelines to tell us what to do.

Keep your guidelines short in number and in description. Four or five clear, positively worded statements should suffice. If students have poor working memory or attention spans, they will not be able to remember more rules than that. If guidelines could be boiled down to:

1. Follow directions
2. Keep everyone safe
3. Show respect to all

That might be enough.

A code word or phrase that warns when something inappropriate has just happened could be created. For put-downs or micro-aggressions,

"Oops-ouch!" "Excuse me, what?" or "New choice!" can act as reminders that the offender is headed in the wrong direction, but that there is still time to stop. No one is being accused of being inappropriate or bad, so no one needs to feel as if they are being put on the spot. If there are other types of distraction, like talking out of turn or two students having a side conversation, a different code word or phrase can be devised.

If students start to use quips or micro-aggressions to gain laughs for themselves and put another student down, or they do not respond to your reminder, do not let their behavior go on. Call a "freeze" in the action. A good way to start addressing what was just said or done is to say:

> I'm feeling uncomfortable, and I'm not really sure why. Let's talk about this. Does anyone else feel uncomfortable?

This opens the discussion up to the group to identify what and why an action was not a great idea. Then the onus for appropriate behavior is not just on the teacher, it becomes valued conduct for the whole class. Try to run these discussions without blame; define them for the students as "teachable moments." Don't frame these kinds of discussions for yourself as a waste of time; they are not! Think of them as the start of bystander intervention practice. Students get the opportunity to reflect on their behavior and put themselves in other people's shoes (the beginning of learning empathy), while treating each other with warmth and respect. In addition, the following executive functions are being exercised: Self-reflection (part of metacognition) and inhibition (part of emotional and behavioral regulation).

Of course, if the guidelines are not followed, there must be a potential consequence in place. A simple, straightforward consequence could be:

> If anyone is offended or hurt by something that we do, then we can't do [whatever game or activity is being played]. We will have to stop and sit down.

Inclusion

The drama games and explorations in this book will be successful whether you are working solely with students in a special education classroom, in a neurotypical classroom, or in an inclusive classroom. One of the wonderful aspects of drama is that it levels the playing field. Often, neurodiverse students can participate as well and as creatively as their neurotypical peers. However, there are times when adaptations need to be made to instructions or games, and this will be addressed in this section.

Working together on arts projects can be a wonderful way for students with and without disabilities to get to know and appreciate each other. As appreciation is built, so are social connections and friendships. In fact, if an inclusive class is not functioning in an inclusive manner, working together through the arts, especially drama because of its social aspects, helps break down barriers between students.

Creating Inclusive Attitudes

Humans cannot help creating categories of people who are like "us" and not like us ("them"). This is the intrinsic way our brains developed to take in and process information. New people and information are sorted into "similar" and "unsimilar." Anything that is in the "similar" category is accepted or learned through assimilation. People and information in the "unsimilar" category are either rejected, forgotten, or incorporated through accommodation (Flavell, 1963). This learning is done unconsciously, beneath our level of awareness. What we often do become aware of when something is "unsimilar" is a feeling of discomfort or threat. The more different a person or idea is from what we have previously experienced, the more threatening the feeling is (Casey & Robinson, 2017).

Our brains are amazingly quick. At the unconscious level they can process 11 million bits of information every second. They can register if another person is male or female within 50 milliseconds, if their racial background is different in 100 milliseconds, and in 200 milliseconds our brains can decipher if a face is familiar or not. All this happens beneath our level of awareness; we become conscious of it later (Casey & Robinson, 2017). Contrast the power of our mind's unconscious level with our con-scious one, which can only handle 40–50 bits of information a second (Kwong, 2020). The processing that goes on at the unconscious level is called System 1 thinking (fast), and conscious processing is called System 2 thinking (slow) (Kahneman, 2011).

Those who grow up in a family and community where we are exposed to few "different" others on a daily basis will naturally hesitate when they first come into close contact with someone who is unsimilar in some way.

This is true whether the differentness is due to physical difference (color of skin, use of wheelchair, extremely thick glasses, hearing aids, very short stature, etc.), observable behaviors (religious customs or dress, language or accent, awkward gait, seizures, slurred speech, tics, stimming, etc.), or other types of observable differences (lower than normal academic abilities, inability to make eye contact, awkward social skills). No one has to tell us to avoid getting close to this new person. Our System 1 thinking, working away outside of our consciousness, identifies them not only as a stranger, but also as *strange,* and therefore most likely not to be trusted. This is called *implicit bias,* because we are unaware of it.

We pick up this wariness not just because of the way our brain is taking in the differences below our awareness, but also from observing the behavior of trusted others and listening to what they say about those differences. We pay attention to media and all aspects of our culture – how could we not? It's everywhere! These incorporated Level 2 judgments add up to *confirmation bias*, the tendency to look for ways to confirm our preexisting beliefs so that we feel we have more solid evidence for our judgments than we actually do (Kahneman, 2011).

Being held at a social distance because of a personal difference has been proven to be literally a hurtful experience. Social psychologist Kipling Williams (2011) studied exclusion for years and discovered that when people are rejected or excluded from a group, their brains register the experience in the circuits of the brain that process physical pain. So much for the old adage, "Sticks and stone may break my bones, but names will never hurt me." Exclusion literally hurts! Moreover:

> …researchers also found that twice daily doses of acetaminophen over three weeks reduced daily reports of distress and hurt feelings from social rejection in 62 students, compared with the effects of a placebo. Together the findings suggest that social rejection and physical injury are not such different experiences and share underlying neural pathways. (2011, p. 33)

Given that we automatically categorize people as "alike" or "not alike," what can be done to get past the rejection that so many "not alike" people receive? How do we get to a place where they are accommodated, accepted, and valued as fellow human beings? The first step, of course, is to educate ourselves about our unconscious brain processes and understand how they work in their default mode. Done!

Then, before we start berating ourselves for categorizing others as "us" or "them," we need to take a minute and stop our inner critics from beating up on us. Self-criticism for something we did not know we were doing is a waste of time and energy. What is important is to become aware of what we were doing and move on to the step that will really make a difference: Learning how to consciously focus on viewing and communicating with people who are "unlike" us in an actively positive manner. By doing that we discover what they have in common with us.

If you overhear negative talk that suggests your students may have created an "in group" and an "out group" (or several "out groups"), one of the worst ways to deal with it is to yell at and shame the biased members of the "in group." It may make you feel vindicated, but doing so only makes the "in group" recipients feel threatened and defensive. Once someone is defensive, they stop listening to anything that contradicts what they already believe (Lichtenberg, van Beusekom, & Gibbons, 1997). Other poor responses include ignoring the problem (problems involving bullying and "othering" or rejection of people never go away, they just fester and get worse), denying the biased person's experience (they will just think you don't understand), or agreeing with them just to make the situation go away (Lichtenberg et al., 1997).

The Pygmalion Effect

The approach that has worked most effectively for me has been to consciously employ the Pygmalion Effect (Rosenthal, 1991). In a social psychology experiment beginning in the '60s, teachers were told that recent tests had identified certain students in their classes as "spurters," who would show significant academic gains during the school year. Interestingly enough, that school year those students *did* experience major gains! However, at year's end, it was revealed that no tests had actually been done – the students identified as "spurters" were randomly chosen. At the beginning of the year, some were "gifted," some were "average," some were "below average." By the end of the year, they were all at the top of their classes. The teachers had communicated through their intentions, attention, words, and actions that the identified students had incredible potential, and the students responded to those expectations with belief, rose to the occasion, and achieved!

This experiment has been replicated many times over the years with the same results. If you believe someone you are teaching has the potential to succeed, you create a self-fulfilling prophecy for them. Is it magic? No. People are always able to sense if someone in authority believes in them, or if they don't. Think back to teachers, coaches, and family members in your life. You knew who believed in you. Those people held a positive image of you in their hearts and in their mind's eye. You felt safe with them. They encouraged you. They created challenges for you that were just at the right level of difficulty to motivate you to work on and surmount them, and when you did, they celebrated your success.

Instead of letting your thoughts unconsciously move students into the plus column (able/worthy/interesting) or the minus column (unable/worthless/boring), choose to consciously see the potential in each of them. This is not a matter of making something up and deluding yourself – you really do not know what each of your students is truly capable of achieving and, probably, neither do they. If their potential – academic and otherwise – is left open as an optimistic possibility, who knows what they can accomplish?

Not only will the Pygmalion Effect you create through your conscious awareness and communication prompt a difference in the attitudes and actions of the individual students who are on the receiving end, it will also change how the students view each other. Students look to their teachers to set the tone of how the classroom community is supposed to function. When they sense that everyone is being actively accepted, generously respected, and enthusiastically valued, they will join in.

Your conscious exercise of the Pygmalion Effect can be supported through generous and heartfelt praise of effort and originality. This does not need to be focused on academics; it can be directed toward contributions made to the group in terms of leadership, citizenship, or support of others. Some people are wonderful listeners; they really take in what is being said. Some people are sensitive to the feelings of others and reach out when they see another feeling alone or sad. There are innumerable actions – big and small – that students can be acknowledged for.

Knowing that someone notices and appreciates what you have done can be a big deal. Showing that appreciation does not need to be done in a showy manner. A pat on the back, a quick note, a wink, a nod of approval may be all that is needed for someone to feel included and valued.

Highlighting Appreciation and Praise

If you think highlighting appreciation and praise would be a valuable addition to your classroom community, here are a few ideas for group appreciation rituals which could be incorporated into your classroom. Make sure that your students are mature enough to do these exercises in the spirit in which they are intended, because opening one's self up to feedback from peers puts students into a vulnerable position. A student who is being silly or sarcastic will destroy any sense of trust in the group.

Circle of Acknowledgment (Thanks to Nancy Sondag and Barbara McKechnie)

Goals addressed: Identifying what is praiseworthy in oneself, Giving genuine praise to another.

Space requirements: Students standing in a circle.

Teacher participation: Coach and participant.

Go around the circle and allow each student to say something they have done in the last week that they are proud of themselves for doing. The class acknowledges their achievement by applauding and cheering.

Circle of Appreciation

Goals addressed: Identifying what is praiseworthy in another, Accepting praise graciously.

Space requirements: Students standing in a circle.

Teacher participation: Coach and participant.

A student takes one step forward (or sits on a chair/stool in the middle of the circle) and the other students go around the circle saying one thing they appreciate about that student. It should not be about physical appearance (things like clothing, hair, facial features, etc.), but about qualities they possess, noteworthy actions they have taken for others, or insights they have shared that helped someone understand something in class.

Notes of Acknowledgment

Goals addressed: Teaching peers how to identify useful and appreciated aspects of work done by another student.

Space requirements: Artwork, poems, stories, papers, or any artifact that has been created and shared in class can be placed on a large table or on the floor so that students can access each.

Teacher participation: Coach and participant.

Students are given small pieces of paper (maybe Post-it notes) and are asked to write a word or a phrase of praise or appreciation about each of the assignments on display. The note might be about how the work affected the student in a positive manner. The notes are signed and left next to or stuck on the assignment.

Greeting Cards

Goals addressed: Encouraging another or congratulating another.

Space requirements: This could be done at students' desks.

Teacher participation: Coach.

Supplies needed: A piece of paper folded in half, markers or crayons, names of all students in a box.

Each student picks the name of another student. They create a greeting card for that person. This might be framed as a card of congratulations or a card of encouragement, depending on what is needed by the person at the moment.

Manito (Do-Gooder) (Aycox, 1999)

Goals addressed: Showing appreciation for another.

Space required: This could be done at students' desks or gifts could be made at home.

Teacher participation: Coach.

Supplies needed: Variety of art supplies, names of students in a box.

This is an activity that is similar to Secret Santa, except that it is done at a time of the year that has no holiday. Each person picks the name of another. This will be the person they will do good deeds for and give non-commercial, homemade gifts to secretly during the designated time for the game. The time could span several days, a week, two weeks, or a month. The Manitos try to keep their identities a secret. They may give small home-made gifts to their person, drawings, pieces of candy (if that is allowed in the classroom), provide certificates for services (like carrying their person's lunch tray after the revelation of Manitos), etc. The Manitos are revealed at the end of the designated time in a special ceremony where one last gift is given.

Superhero Capes

Goals addressed: Excellent closure activity for the year or at the completion of a major group project.

Space requirements: Enough room for everyone to move around to write on each other's capes. (Usually long lines get formed with people writing on each other's backs.)

Teacher participation: Coach and participant.

Supplies required: Large sheets of newsprint or butcher paper cut to the appropriate size of students' backs (the shorter side should go from shoulder to shoulder and the longer side should go down the back to about the middle of the thighs), a colored magic marker for each student, two pieces of masking tape per piece of paper.

Students help each other by taping the "superhero capes" to the back of their peers at the shoulders. When everyone has a cape, students go around and write a message of appreciation on the cape or draw pictures and sign them. No one can see what people have written until everyone is done, and they take off the capes.

Helpful Hint: Prepare for this ritual by ripping off the lengths of masking tape before the activity and attaching them to the side of a table or a corner, so students can easily take two pieces of tape and a piece of paper to find another person to help "cape."

Creating Inclusive Drama Explorations and Experiments

Accommodations and adaptations are sometimes needed in order to make drama games and explorations accessible. Depending on whether you are working with a special education class or an inclusive class, you may need to adjust certain aspects of the game. Many changes for accessibility are simple and inexpensive. Often students or their parents can offer ideas that have worked in situations outside of school. If you have a gym teacher, recreation instructor, physical therapist, or occupational therapist at your school who is good at making accommodations, you could ask them for suggestions. I have found that most of the time accommodations are a matter of thinking practically and going for the simplest version of a game or adjusting the rules so students have less items to remember or manipulate. The less you and your students have to think about in terms of extraneous words or actions, and the more they can focus on the game, the better. After you have adapted a few games, you will start to get the hang of it. In the meantime, what follows are general suggestions.

Wheelchairs

Keep in mind that wheelchairs make mobility possible. Often when someone is in a wheelchair they are thought of as unable to move. Not true! The wheelchair has made mobility possible. If the wheelchair is motorized, the user of the chair should be relatively independent. The only time help might be needed is if the student was unable to move the chair themselves.

In a circle game in which people change places (a popular game configuration), instead of having everyone sit in chairs, mark each person's space on the floor with a piece of masking tape. Have mobile students stand on the tape. The person(s) in the wheelchair(s) park(s) over a piece of tape. When players move to a new space, it is clear where everyone can go.

Be sure that any opening needed for an activity is wider than the width of the largest chair (usually 32 inches). If tables are too short for students' chairs to pull up under them, blocks of wood can be put underneath the legs to raise the tabletop high enough to fit the wheelchair arms underneath. A clearance of at least 30 inches is usually needed. If there are worries about the table legs getting knocked off the blocks, power tools can create a recess in the middle of the block the size of the leg bottom (leaving a lip around the edge) to anchor it in place.

Any ramp used to access a raised space needs to have a rise of 8.3 percent (a one foot rise for every 12 feet in length). A rise of more than 8.3 percent will make the slope so steep that any non-motorized the wheelchair will have a tendency to roll backwards down the ramp. Not a particularly pleasant or safe experience for the person using the chair! Another important ramp requirement is to be at least 36 inches wide (i.e., wider than the chair) and to have raised lips along both sides, so the chair cannot fall off.

Autism Spectrum Disorder

Students who have autism sometimes have difficulty letting go of what they know to be "the truth" or "reality," in order to use their imaginations with others. For instance, in a game in which neurotypical students decide they want to act as if they are magical creatures like a talking frog or a unicorn, a student with Autism Spectrum Disorder (ASD) might refuse to play along because, "Frogs can't talk," and "There is no such thing as a unicorn," or more forcefully put, "Unicorns and talking frogs are lies!"

Chapter Four introduces the improvisation rule of "Yes, and…" During improvisations, actors must accept whatever their fellow actors create and then build on it. A beginning student with ASD may struggle with that rule. One way to deal with this could be to start with very realistic characters and improvisations. Once your students on the spectrum begin to enjoy acting, there is a much better chance they will become willing to make the transition into imaginary worlds that others create.

On the other hand, if students with ASD love science and science fiction, there may be no difficulty as far as they are concerned with imagining fanciful creatures, but there may be a rigidity of only wanting to act out one character or one type of situation. For instance, a young boy who only wants to act out a dog may insist that he plays a dog in every scene. Many children on and off the spectrum develop favorite characters like princesses, ninjas, or horses that they love acting out repeatedly. This is actually a normal occurrence in a drama class with elementary-aged children. There is nothing wrong with allowing that dog to be in a number of scenes. After a while, you can begin to request that the student acts out dogs with different kinds of qualities or personalities instead of the same dog with the same personality. Drama and play therapists call this "adding a discrepancy." If the student wants to know why, say that it is important to stretch acting skills and learn how to create different kinds of characters. You will probably find that eventually, the student volunteers for a different kind of role. This is the beginning of flexibility. The process may take some time, but be patient, and when it finally occurs, be cool about it.

Tactile Defensiveness

Students who have attention deficit hyperactivity disorder or autism spectrum disorder may be tactilely defensive. This means they are sensitive to being touched, especially with a light touch or a tag that might be used in some games. There may be students with these conditions or others who feel uncomfortable holding hands. Most of the games described in this book do not involve touch, and if they do, suggestions will accompany the game for how to deal with it as a helpful hint. Generally, if holding hands is important in playing the game, in place of touching, students could hold short scarves or bandanas between them to create connection.

Executive Functioning

Many of the difficulties that students with learning disabilities have relate to their executive functioning: processes such as working memory, sequencing, attention, focus, and organization in thinking. The games in Chapter Two and Three provide practice for the improvement of many executive functions. These games, worked on carefully, will help students who struggle with these difficulties improve over time.

Sensory Integration

Some students with cognitive or developmental disabilities also have processing issues related to sensory integration, such as balance, orientation in space, or overstimulation of their senses. Warm-up games with constantly changing movements and noises that are passed around in irregular patterns will be confusing to them. Instead of playing these types of games, plan to start with simple go-around games where each person in the circle takes a turn in order. If players are not ready to be put on the spot to respond solo, there are games that require unison work or small group interactions. Games with more complexity or speed can be added slowly as the class develops trust, group cohesion, more sensory integration, and comfort with activities.

If a student is easily overwhelmed by noise, an inexpensive set of headphones from a hardware store will lower sound levels enough so they can participate comfortably and still hear. Certain awareness activities can be designed to allow students to focus on just one sense at a time (Change Three can be adapted to Change One). This helps these students learn the game while training their senses to respond to only one sense at a time. Occupational therapists and speech pathologists are excellent resources to turn to for accommodation ideas about sensory integration and executive functioning.

Talking About Differences

When considering peer-to-peer relationships, many typically-abled students are unwilling to engage with classmates who have a visible disability due to a feeling of discomfort, fear of being offensive, or a perceived lack of experience interacting with someone with a disability (Shah, Wallace, Conor, & Kiszley, 2015). In order for teachers and their students to focus on issues of access and equity, it is critical that they engage students in conversations regarding disability and promote ableism awareness in their environment.

(Bialka, 2017, p. 174)

If you find you are in a situation like the one described above, and neurotypical students are hesitant to interact with neurodiverse students, or there is unspoken discomfort of some kind, it becomes important to just sit down and hash it out. One way to start a conversation like this is to say:

We all have different abilities that allow us to excel and different challenges that sometimes we need help with. I _____. [Say something that you actually do need help with – it might be as simple, as "I am new at doing drama, so I need you to listen closely and follow my directions."]

Then go around the classroom and ask everyone to share what kind of help they need and how others can help them. This way everyone has opened up and been a little vulnerable.

I have found that after an initial discussion like this, if students are still not working together, it can be useful to sit them down and ask directly:

Why are you having trouble working together? Let's figure out what we can do to:

- Communicate with each other better
- Stop bumping into each other
- Be more sensitive to each other's feelings
- Or whatever you intuit the problem is based on

While the source of the problem is important to identify, ultimately it is more important to figure out as a group how to overcome it.

Sometimes adults avoid talking straightforwardly to children about what they are socially struggling with, not wanting to "put them on the spot" or thinking that they will not have the insight to know what is going wrong. However, sometimes, children know exactly what the problem is, but they will not tell you until you ask them calmly and directly. Sometimes I think they are trying to protect the adults who they think can't see or understand the problem. Opening up the discussion to the whole group, can get the real problems out in the open. If blaming others starts, stop it with:

> No one needs to be blamed for anything. I want to know what actions each person can take to help solve the problem. We can't control other peoples' behavior; we can only control our own. What can *you* do to make the situation better?

Economic psychologist Paul J. Zak has discovered that when we show respect for each other, play together, and laugh together, we release oxytocin, a feel-good hormone, into our brain and body. It motivates us to expand our social network, make friends, and reach out to others in positive ways (Zak, 2012). A "virtuous cycle" is created in which oxytocin generates feelings of respect, trust, and empathy. Those social experiences lead to cooperation, connection, and sharing, which, in turn, lead to more oxytocin and that leads to more…you get the picture (Zak, 2012). Allow the joy of working together on creative projects to weave a web of kindness throughout your classroom.

Why Make Time in Your Teaching Schedule for Drama?

In today's education system, teachers are overwhelmed with paperwork, meetings, and curriculum requirements from every side. Adding additional activities to their class schedule becomes difficult, no matter how useful they may be. So why take the time to incorporate the dramatic games and explorations provided in this book into your lesson plans? There are a number of reasons: Drama can motivate students to engage in learning, create a more internal locus of control, support the development of executive functions, emotional regulation, and social skills, and drama is a form of embodied learning.

Deeper Engagement in Learning

Engagement in school with the curriculum and with the school community is the first step in getting students to commit to learning. Three basic psychological needs have been identified as requirements for engagement: relatedness, autonomy, and competence (Osterman, 2000; Ryan & Deci, 2000). Let's take a look at each of these requirements.

Relatedness

Humans, being social animals, want to feel welcome in an environment, especially if they have to spend many hours there every day. While socialization is not and cannot be the primary function of school, it can be the glue that keeps students wanting to come back. For relatedness to develop, some quality time needs to be spent making connections. Since recess has been cut in many schools, lunch remains the only time when students can socialize. That limits the amount of time and the number of peers one person can get to know, especially if you have a group of friends that you always sit with.

Much better group connections can be formed if students are engaged in cooperative activities that allow them to interact with the whole group instead of a small sub-set of friends. This does not mean that a mixer game must always be played; however, the more positive contacts that are made among peers and with the teacher, the wider the sociometric net grows to include the entire classroom community. Whenever I begin with a new group, I make sure that I plan a variety of games that involve the whole group, pairs, and small groups, and I make sure students rotate into different pairs and small groups, so that by the end of several weeks, they have worked with everyone in the class more than once in different configurations.

Autonomy

Autonomy comes into play when students are doing drama because even in a collaborative game like Machines (see page 120), everyone has their part to play to make the group successful. Positive attention and feelings of self-efficacy are created when students participate in improvisational scenes. A problem needs to be solved or an obstacle must be overcome for one character or a group of characters to achieve their goal. Since the scene is unscripted, many of the solutions come spontaneously out of the action in the moment. (There will be more about improvisation in Chapter Four.) How wonderful to demonstrate one's cleverness and intelligence in front of one's peers and be appreciated for it!

Autonomy links into creating a more internal locus of control or belief in one's ability to make changes effectively in one's life (Nowicki, 2016). Locus of control is measured on a scale from 0 to 40. The lower the score, the more internal one is; the higher the score, the more external. Extreme scores on either end of the scale are not helpful for a person as they indicate inflexibility in thinking (Nowicki, 2016).

Locus of control scores do not necessarily stay the same most of one's life. They can be changed through experience. For instance:

> ...for Internality to develop sufficiently, children need an appropriately safe environment in which they can feel secure, nurtured, and supported. Within such settings, they are encouraged to explore and interact with their surroundings to gain awareness of what they can and can't control....they must have their behavior consistently and contingently reinforced by others.
>
> (Nowicki, 2016, p. 213)

Students who have a more internal locus of control have been shown consistently to have better academic success (Nowicki, 2016). That means, they believe that what they do directly affects the amount they learn, and the grades they earn: reading, paying attention in class, doing homework, studying for tests are all actions you can choose to take to achieve success. No one else can do it for you. Students with an external locus of control do not believe their efforts make any difference. They feel helpless. They see themselves as being given grades, not earning them. Their belief about being powerless to change what happens to them guides them to assume that it would not matter how much they studied; they would still get a poor grade. If they get a good grade, they assume it is due to luck or because the test was easy. In contrast, Internal locus of control creates intrinsic motivation; the student is choosing to persist in their efforts to learn, not looking for an external reward. Drama activities teach students that when they take action, something happens. They are capable of making change and making a difference.

Competence

A third psychological need for engagement in school is competence. Students feel competent when they are able to do something well and when they get positive feedback on the work they have done. Most students will feel competent in drama very quickly because, as mentioned earlier, it is a natural learning tool that everyone has used before. The only times I have had difficulty getting someone involved in drama has been when that person was either extremely shy to the point of social phobia or when a person was deeply depressed and grieving a major loss. Most likely once students become engaged in drama, they will be more motivated to engage with other parts of the classroom community.

Meaning-Making

Ross Anderson (2018) suggests a fourth psychological need for engagement should be added to the above three: meaning-making. He believes students will engage deeply in their education if they have the opportunity to explore the concepts within their curriculum by using their whole being (senses, body, cognition, and emotions) with the end goal of generating their own metaphors and solutions to problems that make personal meaning for themselves. This requires enough time, space, and support by the classroom community to actively create the appropriate learning environment. He suggests drama as the perfect platform for allowing meaning-making to emerge. Rather than being an abstract concept that must be memorized, students' knowledge becomes a felt reality that then can be remembered more easily. Students can share their meaningful metaphors with each other, revealing different representations and perspectives of the material they have been working together to understand. Anderson reports the example of a sixth grade student illustrating the scientific process of evaporation by enacting a grape drying up into a raisin in the hot afternoon sun. This student contributed a meaningful and memorable image to her classmates through her own creativity and problem solving. She will not forget what evaporation is, and neither will they.

Tackling Executive Functioning Deficits

Many of the drama games and improvisations in this book work to improve executive functioning: the capability to organize, categorize, and work with information. "Executive functions allow us to use top-down cognitive skills to intentionally initiate behavior that moves us toward selected goals" (Norman, 2020). If students' executive functioning is poor, they will not be able to pay attention, follow a sequence of directions, organize a learning task, or control impulsive behavior. Executive functioning, to be described in more detail in the next chapter, directs the cognitive tasks of learning and problem solving as well as emotional and behavioral regulation.

Digital Media's Effect on Executive Functions

Deficits in executive functioning are often found in students who have learning and neurological differences, but in the past 20 years dysfunctions have been discovered in neurotypical students as well. The cause is believed to be their growing use of digital devices. In 2017, Common Sense Media reported that children between the age group of zero to eight spent two and quarter hours per day on screens: smartphones, tablets, or TVs. That is almost 16 hours a week. Forty-two percent of them had their own tablet (Rideout, 2017). In 2019, children between the age group of 8–12 were reported by Common Sense Media to spend 4 hours and 44 minutes per day: over 33 hours per week. Fifty-three percent have their own smart phone by the age of 11 and more than sixty-nine percent do by 12 (Rideout & Robb, 2019). If that was the amount in 2017 and 2019, respectively, imagine what it is now in the middle of the COVID-19 pandemic! (At this writing more recent statistics for these age groups are not available.)

The electronic media students interact with daily from iPads to smartphones and from the Internet to eBooks take a toll on their ability to sustain attention and block out distractions, control their impulses, retain information, self-reflect, think critically, analyze, and use their imaginations (Ioannidis, Hook, Goudriaan, Vlies, Fineberg, Grant, & Chamberlain, 2019; Landon-Murray & Anderson, 2013; Loh & Kanai, 2016). The brain is like other parts of the body: if you do not use one of its skills, you lose that skill. In this case, all the quick shifts of attention, repeated visual changes, and the constant flow of different information of electronic media reformats aspects of our brains (Carr, 2011; Ioannidis et al., 2019; Landon-Murray &

Anderson, 2013; Loh & Kanai, 2016). Not enough research has been done to show exactly how the brain is effected, but behavior changes indicate brain changes.

While children can learn information from TV and digital media, there is a transfer deficit of as much as 50%. That means children learn better when they interact with live, three-dimensional people and material (Barr, 2019). Transfer deficit is less if the online platform is interactive, but it is never as good as in-person teaching or joint media engagement with an adult (Barr, 2019).

The more often students use digital media and the Internet at home and school, the more aspects of their executive functioning are compromised. They need to practice activities that increase the executive functions they are not exercising while on digital media. The best time and place to do this is while they are in school with their teacher who can provide the appropriate kind and amount of practice.

Interventions for Improvement of Executive Functions

Psychologists Adele Diamond and Daphne Ling (2016) have reviewed research on interventions that claim to improve executive functions and have found that many of the touted computer and physical exercise programs are ineffective. However, they do find that traditional Tae-Kwon-Do, yoga, mindfulness, and training in theatre improve executive functions. One reason for this is that these methods require dedicated practice of difficult tasks that are constantly being varied and which use equal parts of physical and cognitive challenge (Diamond & Ling, 2016). I am not an expert at Tae-Kown-Do, yoga, or mindfulness, but I do know how to implement interventions through theatre!

Play has been identified as a way to develop executive functions. Jaak Panksepp, a neuroscientist who created the field of affective neuroscience, identified one of the seven basic emotional systems as PLAY. PLAY originates in the brain stem and wires the limbic and pre-cortex together (Brown & Vaughn, 2009). This, Panksepp says, creates "the possibility that one of the long term functions of social play is to promote maturation of various higher brain areas, including frontal cortical ones" (Panksepp et al., 2003, p.103–104). The activated subcortical PLAY system seems to particularly facilitate the development of the executive function of inhibition, which is crucial for behavioral regulation. All of the other emotional systems

(SEEKING, LUST, CARING, RAGE, FEAR, and PANIC) can be brought into the PLAY system to "play around with" and learn about (Panksepp, 1998).

> ...in higher organisms, play may encourage organisms to test the perimeters of their knowledge. In short, the brain's PLAY networks may help stitch individuals into the social fabric that is the staging ground for their lives. Is it any wonder, then, that play is such fun – perhaps one of the major brain sources of joy?
>
> (Panksepp, 1998, pp. 280–281)

Why not use that source of joy as a motivation for learning and practicing complex higher brain processes? Panksepp says it best:

> Of course, the bottom line is that play is such fun. If we were able to make the process of learning more playful, the whole enterprise of education might become easier.
>
> (Panksepp, 1998, p. 297)

Incorporating Embodied Cognition in Your Teaching

The first kind of learning we engage in as infants is exploring the world through our bodies and our senses. The sensory-motor stage of development (ages zero to two) is followed by the pre-operational stage from two to seven. In this second stage, we add learning through imitation, dramatic play, verbalizing thinking, using objects symbolically, and role-play (Flavell, 1963). Both of these early stages involve embodied cognition. We literally take actions with our bodies in order to learn.

When the Piaget's developmental stages of childhood are taught in Child Psychology, the impression that students often take away is that children "graduate" from one stage to the other. In students' minds, moving into the pre-operational stage means the period of sensory-motor learning is finished, and moving into the concrete operational stage means dramatic play and role-play is traded in for the use of inner cognitive skills. In actuality, early stages do not go away, and we do not "graduate" from one stage to the other; we add new options for learning to the older ones as our brains mature.

Figure 1.1 on page 32 shows how each developmental stage rests upon the others. Notice that lower stages are wider than the stages above them,

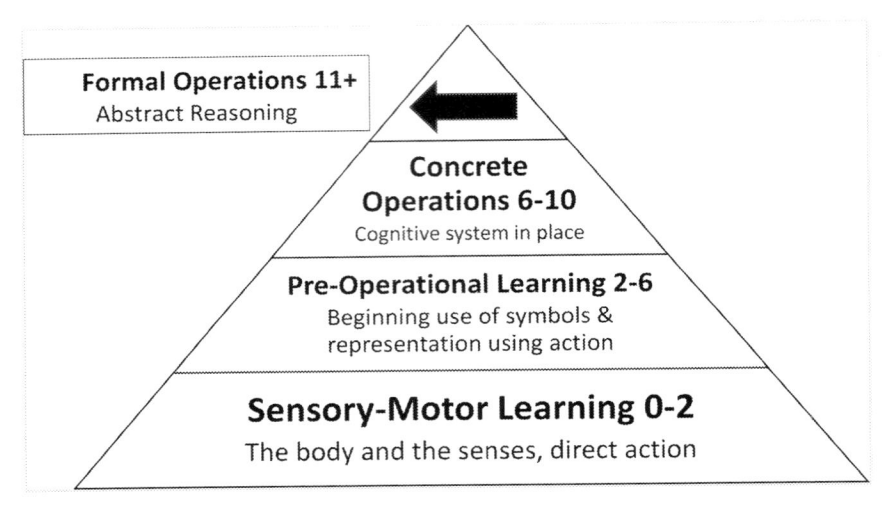

Figure 1.1 Pyramid of Piaget's learning development.

indicating that they are the base for the next level of development. They do not disappear; they remain as part of the skill-set the child, and later adult, has at their disposal. If the developmental stages are framed in this way, embodied cognition clearly can be seen as a major support system for learning.

Embodied cognition uses all of the external and internal senses, movement, and affective states of students to act out or demonstrate an abstract academic concept, object, or event (Kontra, Goldin-Meadow, & Beilock, 2012). Said another way, "important cognitive functions are essentially grounded in action and perception as a function of experience" (Kiefer & Trumpp, 2012, p. 15). When the body is used as a learning tool, the student is actively employing their sensorimotor, physiological, cognitive, and affective experience to integrate the information. Their attention is captivated on all levels, and they tend to stay in the here and now, focused on the lesson. Because of their active involvement, as they use more aspects of themselves, there is a better chance that the information will be understood at a deeper level, comprehended more thoroughly, and may have a greater chance of being encoded into long term memory.

A review of research done on embodied learning of abstract concepts in comparison with traditional instruction methods between 2003 and 2013 demonstrated significant learning gains for participants who were using full-body interaction. The full-body interactions also involved participants emotionally, and this motivated them to work harder (Malinverni & Pares, 2014).

In expanding more deeply on how embodied cognition works, Chandler and Tricot (2015) say it is

> ...explained by two mechanisms: enriched encoding and more efficient use of working memory subsystems. With regard to enriched encoding explanation, it is assumed that taking action in response to information, in addition to simply seeing or hearing it, can provide the memory with additional cues with which to represent and retrieve the acquired knowledge. With regard to the explanation of more efficient use of the limited capacity working memory, it is assumed that dividing the cognitive load imposed by a learning task across different working memory subsystems (i.e., visual, auditory, and motor) can prevent negative effects of too high a load on one specific subsystem. (p. 366)

Using the body increases blood flow, which then moves more oxygen into the brain to use for learning. In addition, movement of the body releases brain proteins like brain-derived neurotrophic factor (BDNF) and nerve-growth factor (NGF) that encourage the growth of neurons (Chandler & Tricot, 2015).

Drama can be incorporated into the teaching of science, history, language, reading, and even mathematics. They become more memorable for students by making them more concrete and comprehensible. Chapter Five will go into detail about how this use of drama can be brought into your classroom in small or large amounts. The more you start thinking dramatically, the easier it is to invent new ways to bring all of your lessons to life. But let's not jump ahead. Chapter Two is designed to start you and your students out on the right path to using drama as a tool for improving your students' abilities to learn, specifically in relation to their executive functioning.

Assessing Success

In today's schools, teachers and counselors are often required to prove that their educational and counseling methods are achieving success. Without evidence, administrators often will not give their blessing to new ways of working. There are no sure-fire, simple pencil and paper instruments that exist to prove students' executive functioning, empathy, or communication skills have improved or that students have become internally motivated to learn, engaged in their studies, and deeply engaged in school. If there were, they would be employed in classrooms all the time to prove that many other pedagogical improvements work. In fact, they probably would be part of the heavy administrative load being shouldered by teachers already.

One Simple Measurement: Spectrograms

One simple way to measure change in the atmosphere and emotional connection within your classroom is to create a pre- and post-intervention spectrogram. Before you start implementing drama, pass out a list of the names of everyone in your class to every student. Ask them to put a checkmark next to the name of all the students they would be willing to work with on a project. Have them fold their paper up, put it in an envelope with their name on it, and pass it up to the front of the room. After six months, pass the same list out again and ask students to put a checkmark next to the name of every student they would be willing to work with on a project. If there are more checkmarks by the names of more people, then your class has developed more positive relationships with each other, trust, and a sense of belonging together.

If you get interested in analyzing this data further you can create a chart like the one below on which to see how many choices have been made. Blacken the box which has the same name in it horizontally and vertically (a person can't choose themselves). Put an X in a box that the student has chosen (across the horizontal line from the chooser's name). If you add the number of X's in the row, you see how many choices each student made. If you add the number of X's in a column, you can see how many choices each student received.

In Figure 1.2, Joe, June, and Natalie have each chosen three others in the group, but they have not been chosen by as many back. Only Joe has chosen someone (Bill) who has also chosen him. While Julie feels disconnected from the class the most (she has not chosen anyone), she is liked by at least three others who have chosen her.

CHOSEN

	Names	Bill	Phil	Joe	Sam	June	Julie	Kamala	Molly	Natalie	T
C	Bill	■		X	X						2
H	Phil	X	■		X						1
O	Joe	X	X	■	X						3
O	Sam		X		■						1
S	June					■	X	X		X	3
E	Julie						■				0
R	Kamala						X	■	X		2
S	Molly		X				X		■		2
	Natalie						X	X	X	■	3
	TOTAL	**2**	**2**	**2**	**3**	**1**	**3**	**2**	**2**	**1**	

Figure 1.2 Chart showing sociometric choices of students in a fictional class at the beginning of a year. Far right total along horizonal line shows number of choices made by person in far left box. Bottom total shows how many people chose the person whose name is in the top box. There is not yet much social connection among class members.

If the class comes to trust each other more through working and playing together over time, the second chart might look more like this in Figure 1.3. It looks like Sam is the only child who still feels disconnected from the group. Once again, he has made only one choice, but at least he has a

CHOSEN

	Names	Bill	Phil	Joe	Sam	June	Julie	Kamala	Molly	Natalie	T
C	Bill	■	X	X	X		X	X			5
H	Phil	X	■	X	X	X		X			4
O	Joe	X	X	■	X	X			X	X	6
O	Sam		X		■						1
S	June	X		X		■	X	X		X	5
E	Julie		X				■	X	X	X	4
R	Kamala	X		X		X		■	X		4
S	Molly			X			X	X	■	X	4
	Natalie	X			X	X	X	X	X	■	6
	TOTAL	**5**	**4**	**5**	**4**	**4**	**4**	**6**	**4**	**4**	

Figure 1.3 Chart showing sociometric choices of students from the same fictional class shown in Figure 1.2. It is now November, after they have begun to get to know each other through drama activities. The far right total along horizontal line shows number of choices made by person in far left box. Bottom total shows how many people chose the person whose name is in the top box of that column. The class has started to make more connections with each other, although one student in particular appears to be disconnected from the group.

mutual choice with Joe. Kamala has been chosen by six other students: boys *and* girls. Bill and Joe have been chosen by five others, also boys and girls. Joe and Natalie have both chosen six others. Four out the five choices Joe made have chosen him back. This chart shows the class has made progress in developing closer ties with each other. And now instead of most boys choosing only other boys, and most girls choosing only other girls, boys and girls are feeling comfortable with each other.

Another Simple Measure: Ability to Identify Emotions

If you give quizzes on reading comprehension in your language arts class, add a few questions to each quiz about what characters were feeling at certain points in the story. If more students begin to correctly identify characters' emotions over time, the drama exercises involving recognition of emotions (Chapter Two) are bearing fruit. If their emotional vocabulary grows from a narrow range of choices (e.g., mad, sad, glad or good, bad, OK) to more expressive words (e.g., disappointed, frustrated, shocked) they have begun to gain a deeper and more subtle understanding of emotions.

Other Increased Executive Functions

If students who have had difficulty paying attention begin to become more engaged in projects, instead of becoming easily distracted, those students' attenuation abilities have improved. If students who never completed assignments in a timely manner, begin doing so, their concentration abilities have improved. When you notice a change in the behavior of students who used to easily get into fights, their emotional and behavioral regulation is starting to improve.

Will all these wonderful changes transpire after two weeks of drama? No. I am not suggesting cognitive, emotional, and behavioral change is as easy as that! However, I am sure you will see a difference over time, and the more comfortable *you* become at incorporating drama and improvisation into your classroom, the more regularly you will see those kinds of changes appear.

References

Anderson, R. C. (2018). Creative engagement: Embodied metaphor, the affective brain, and meaningful learning. *Mind, Brain, and Education, 12*(2), pp. 72–81.

Aycox, F. (1997) Games we should play in school, 2nd ed. Front Row Experience.

Barr, R. (2019). Growing up in the digital age. *Current Directions in Psychological Science, 28*(4), pp. 341–346.

Bialka, C. S. (2017). Fortifying the foundation: Tools for addressing disability within the multicultural classroom. *Multicultural Perspectives, 19*(3), pp. 172–177.

Brown, S., & Vaughan, C. (2009). *Play: How it shapes the brain, opens the imagination, and invigorates the soul.* Penguin Group.

Carr, N. (2011). *The shallows: What the Internet is doing to our brains.* W. W. Norton.

Casey, M. E., & Robinson, S.M. (2017). *Neuroscience of inclusion: New skills for new times.* Outskirts Press.

Chandler, P., & Tricot, A. (2015). Mind your body: The essential role of body movements in children's learning. *Educational Psychology Review, 27,* pp. 365–370.

Diamond, A., & Ling, D. S. (2016). Conclusions about interventions, programs, and approaches for improving executive functions that appear justified and those that, despite much hype, do not. *Developmental Cognitive Neuroscience 18,* pp. 34–48. Available at: http://dx.doi.org/10.1016/j.dcn.2015.11.005

Flavell, J. H. (1963). *The developmental psychology of Jean Piaget.* D. Van Nostrand Company.

Ioannidis, K., Hook, R. Goudriaan, A. E., Vlies, S., Fineberg, N. A., Grant, J. E., & Chamberlain, S. R. (2019). Cognitive deficits in problematic internet use: Meta-analysis of 40 studies. *The British Journal of Psychiatry, 215,* pp. 639–646. Available at: http//dx.doi.org.10.1192/bjp.2019.3

Kahneman, D. (2011). *Thinking, fast and slow.* Farrar, Straus and Giroux.

Kiefer, M., & Trumpp, N. M. (2012). Embodiment theory and education: The foundations of cognition in perception and action. *Trends in Neuroscience and Education, 1,* pp.15–20. Available at: http//dx.doi.org/10.1016/j.tine.201207.002

Kontra, C., Goldin-Meadow, S., & Beilock, S. L. (2012). Embodied learning across the life span. *Topics in Cognitive Science, 4,* pp. 731–739. Available at: http//dx.doi.org.10.1111/j.1756-8765.2012.01221.x

Kwong, E. (2020, July 15). Understanding unconscious bias. National Public Radio Interview with Pragya Agarwal https://www.npr.org/transcripts/891140598

Landon-Murray, M., & Anderson I. (2013, Fall) Thinking in 140 characters: The Internet, neuroplasticity, and intelligence analysis, *Journal of Strategic Security, 6*(3), pp. 73–82. Available at: http://dx.doi.org/10.5038/1944-0472.6.3.7

Lichtenberg, P., van Beusekom, J., & Gibbons, D. (1997). *Encountering bigotry: Befriending projecting persons in everyday life.* Jason Aronson, Inc.

Loh, K. K., & Kanai, R. (2015) How has the Internet reshaped human cognition? *The Neuroscientist 22*(5), pp. 506–520. Available at: http//dx.doi:10.1177/1073858415595005

Malinverni, L., & Pares, N. (2014). Learning of abstract concepts through full-body interaction: A systemic review. *Educational Technology & Society, 17*(4), pp. 100–116.

Norman, K. (2020, July 25). *The wisdom of play: Theatre games and executive functioning* [Conference session]. American Alliance of Theatre in Education. Online available at: http://www.aate.com/session-block-3

Nowicki, S. (2016). *Choice or chance: Understanding your locus of control and why it matters.* Prometheus Books.

Osterman, K. R. (2000). Students' need for belonging in the school community, *Review of Educational Research, 70*(3), pp. 323–367.

Panksepp, J. (1998). *Affective neuroscience: The foundations of human and animal emotions.* Oxford University Press.

Panksepp, J., Burgdorf, J., Turner, C., & Gordon, N. (2003). Modeling ADHD-type arousal with unilateral frontal cortex damage in rats and beneficial effects of play therapy. *Brain and Cognition, 52,* pp. 97–105.

Patinkin, S. (2000). *The second city: Backstage at the world's greatest comedy theater*. Sourcebooks, Inc.

Piaget, J. (1962). *Play, dreams, and imitation in childhood*. W. W. Norton & Co., Inc.

Rideout, V., & Robb, M. B. (2019). *The Common Sense census: Media use by tweens and teens, 2019*. Common Sense Media. Available at: https://www.commonsensemedia.org/sites/default/files/uploads/research/2019-census-8-to-18-key-findings-updated.pdf

Rideout, V. (2017). *The Common Sense census: Media use by kids age zero to eight*. Common Sense Media. Available at: https://www.commonsensemedia.org/sites/default/files/uploads/research/0-8_executivesummary_release_final_1.pdf

Rosenthal, R. (1991). Teacher expectancy effects: A brief update 25 years after the Pygmalion experiment. *Journal of Research in Education, 1*(1), pp. 3–12.

Rowe, M. B. (1986). Wait time: Slowing down may be a way of speeding up. *Journal of Teacher Education, 37*(1), pp. 43–50.

Ryan, R. M., & Deci, E. L. (2000). Self-determination theory and the facilitation of intrinsic motivation, social development, and well-being. *American Psychologist, 55*(1), 68–78.

Shah, S., Wallis, M., Conor, F., & Kiszely, P. (2015). Bringing disability history alive in schools: Promoting a new understanding of disability through performance methods. *Research Papers in Education, 30*(3), 267–286. http://dx.doi.org/10.1080/02671522.2014.891255

Stahl, R. (1994). Using "Think-Time" and "Wait-Time" skillfully in the classroom. ERIC Digest.

Stanislavski, C. (1948). *An actor prepares*. Theatre Arts Books.

Vygotsky, L. S. (1978). *Mind in society: The development of higher psychological processes*. Harvard University Press.

Vygotsky, L. S. (1986). *Thought and language*. The MIT Press.

Williams, K. D., (2011). The pain of exclusion. *Scientific American Mind, 21*(6), pp. 30–37.

Zak, P. J. (2012). *The moral molecule: How trust works*. Penguin.

Developing Executive Functions Through Drama

Layout of Drama Game Descriptions

Throughout the book, drama games and activities will be described in a similar format. Each will start with the name of the game. If it is known by another name(s), that will be listed in parentheses after it. A list of *goals addressed* will be on the line after the name of the game, followed by *space requirements*. Sometimes the teacher or counselor needs to be a leader or coach who stands outside of the game and gives instructions, like the caller in a Square Dance. Other times they need to play along in the game as a player. This will be indicated after *teacher/counselor participation*.

If there is a requirement for a particular *number of players* (eight players, group divisible by three, groups of five, an even number of players, an odd number of players, etc.), that information will follow space requirements. If there are *supplies needed*, that will be indicated next. Directions for the game will begin in its own paragraph. If there are *variations* or *advanced versions* of the game, those will be included at the end of the main game directions. Please feel free to adapt these games to your specific group and create new variations! Fit the students to the game, rather than the game to the students. There will also be *helpful hints* included as needed.

Executive Functioning

Executive functions consist of cognitive tasks that originate in the prefrontal lobe of the brain. They are crucial for learning; in fact, they guide and structure the learning process and most organizational tasks we undertake in life. In his book *The Executive Brain,* Elkhonon Goldberg says that executive functions are "to the brain what a conductor is to an orchestra, a general is to an army, the chief executive officer is to a corporation" (2009, p. 4). Often students with special needs have poor executive functions in several areas. This can be a problem for regular education students, too.

Executive functioning abilities can be divided into three main categories: Metacognition (which structures thought processes), Emotional Regulation (which structures emotional processes), and Behavior Regulation (which structures the expression of thoughts and emotions through behavior) as shown in Figure 2.1. The abilities in each of these categories interact with each other and often support each other. These categories are not organized in this way by everyone when they discuss executive functioning; however, for the sake of providing clarity, I have made an "executive decision" [pun intended] to organize them this way.

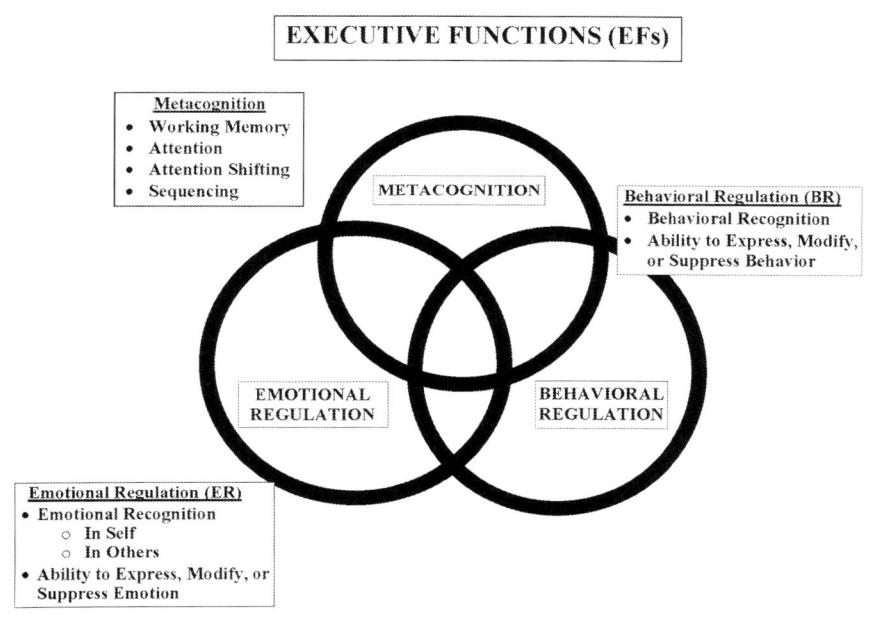

Figure 2.1 The three main categories of Executive Functions with their sub-functions identified.

Within metacognition are the following processes: Working memory, attention, attention shifting, sequencing, task planning, task organizing, task monitoring and evaluation, and self-reflection. This chapter provides games for working memory, attention, attention shifting, and sequencing. These executive functions must be strong before beginning to work on task functions and self-reflection.

Emotional regulation is the ability to recognize emotions in oneself and others and to make choices about how and when to express emotions. Emotions are created in the body, and they affect the body in terms of creating tension or relaxation in muscles and releasing hormones and neurotransmitters into the blood stream, brain, and other organs. They are connected to behavior because many emotions are expressed in words and actions. They are connected to thoughts, as well, which can ramp emotions up or down and allow behaviors to be expressed or to be stopped. An illustration of poor emotional regulation might be when a frustrated student, who is having difficulty with a math problem thinks, "I can't do this!" and angrily throws the math book against the wall. A student with well-developed emotional regulation might respond to the same amount of frustration by thinking, "Calm down, I can figure this out. Relax for a second, and try again." This chapter will focus on games that help students identify emotions in themselves and others and will provide exercises to calm them when they become dysregulated.

Behavior regulation involves choosing to express or inhibit an action. Behavior is always in response to a physical change within the body, in the environment, an emotion, thought, or response to another person's or animal's action. Metacognition, emotional regulation, and behavioral regulation are interwoven with each other. Specific executive functions that integrate all categories include inhibition, initiation, and self-reflection. This chapter will focus on inhibition, also known as impulse control.

Diamond and Ling (2016) have a few words of wisdom about using any intervention to improve emotional functions. First, gains in emotional functioning depend on the amount of time spent practicing them. More is better in terms of frequency and dose. This means it is better to practice three times a week for 15 minutes than once a week for 45 minutes. Even better would be to practice five times a week for 20 minutes! Whenever practice stops, improvement also stops and may even diminish.

The attitude of the leader makes a difference in whether emotional functioning improves (Diamond & Ling, 2016). The leader has to believe whole heartedly in the intervention and be enthusiastic about it. Emotions are contagious! If you are enjoying yourself, there is a good chance that your students will enjoy themselves, too. If you are hesitant or uncomfortable, they will pick up your mood and become uninterested.

Gains in executive functions will stop if students are not continually challenged with more difficulty (Diamond & Ling, 2016). This type of scaffolding is what Vygotsky (1986) called "the zone of proximal development." If students' abilities are always challenged by skills that are just a bit beyond their reach, they will remain engaged and motivated to continue learning. Skills too far above their abilities will frustrate them and cause them to give up; skills at or below their abilities will bore them. This means the leader must watch for the appropriate time to adjust the complexity of a game or exploration.

Students with poor executive functions will demonstrate more improvements than students who already have strong skills. Skills will transfer to other learning situations, but not automatically. Students need to be reminded to make the transfer. In other words, transfer needs to be scaffolded. Look for connections you can help them make between when new skills and opportunities can be put to use. Don't be hesitant to remind students to use a new skill when it would help them. Old habits are hard to change. We automatically do what feels familiar. However, once new skills help students succeed, they will start reminding themselves to implement them.

There are situations outside of the leader's control that could get in the way of gains in executive functioning. Stress, headaches, or a depressed mood will negatively affect executive functions, as will lack of sleep. If students look sleepy or in pain, check to see what is going on at home or school and if there is a way you can help.

The remainder of the chapter consists of a description of specific executive functions in each category, followed by games that help students practice it. Most drama games and activities assist with more than one executive function, and those will be listed in the goals addressed as well. Later, if you cannot remember where in the book a game was described, look in the Game Index at the end of the book where games will be listed in alphabetical order with the page number it can be found on. If you want to find games that assist with a specific executive function, check in the

Appendix which lists all the games and activities alphabetically under each function.

Metacognition

Working Memory

Working memory, called *the chalkboard of the mind* by Daniel Siegel (1999), holds information in awareness so we can consciously think about it. Working memory can only hold information for a short time: As long as the person is focusing on it. As soon as there is an interruption or distraction, the information disappears, and the person starts focusing on the new data coming into working memory.

Psychologists currently believe the average number of chunks (or pieces) of information that can be held in working memory at one time is five plus or minus two chunks (Stein, 2007). The term "chunk" is used instead of "item" or "fact," because some pieces of information are more complex or layered than a single fact, numeral, or letter. Words are made up of letters of the alphabet and often have multiple meanings. Formulae, like $E\text{-}MC^2$, are more complex than the numerals that make them up. Images and pictures are even more complex. Students who have a learning disability that affects working memory or who are anxious or traumatized, will be able to handle less than the average number of chunks. Frequent interruptions cause the chunks in working memory to be lost; in order to begin thinking about the problem again, all those chunks have to be retrieved from long-term memory (Goldberg, 2009).

Swedish neuroscientist Torkel Klingberg (2009) believes that working memory can be improved through training. In fact, "intensive, long-term training on a cognitive task can alter brain activity in much the same way that sensory and motor exercise has been shown to do" (p. 123). However, his experiments have shown that it is effective only "when children work at the limits of their capacity … at least half an hour a day, five days a week for a minimum of five weeks" (p. 126). He also discovered that working memory improves problem-solving abilities. This is because in order to solve a problem, there must be enough room in working memory to hold all the items that are needed to be compared and contrasted.

Here are drama experiments that can improve working memory:

Pass Your Name and a Movement Around the Circle

Goals addressed: Attention, Attention Shifting, Cognitive Flexibility, and Working Memory.

Space requirements: Open space large enough for the class to form a circle.

Teacher/Counselor participation: Player.

Set up: The group stands in a circle. Each person thinks of a motion that either (1) sounds like their first name (e.g., a person named Matt might wipe his feet on an imaginary mat), (2) relates to a quality they have (a student named Susie might have a sparkly personality, so she does jazz hands), or (3) relates to something they like to do (Bill likes to play basketball, so he mimes bouncing a ball and throwing a foul shot). As each person shares their name and motion, the whole group repeats it to help remember it. Make sure each person has a different movement.

Playing: One person starts by saying their name and doing their movement, then says the name and does the movement of someone else. That person says *their* own name and does their movement (to reinforce it for the group), then does the name and movement of someone else. Keep passing the names and movements around the circle randomly until each person has gone several times. Repetition helps us remember information, and when students make associations between the name, appearance, and movement of another person, the name becomes easier to remember.

This is a great game to help a new group get to know each other. Adding the motion in addition to the name creates a moment of embodied learning so there is a visual, auditory and physical component to the memory.

Change Three (Spolin, 1963)

Goals addressed: Attention, Observation Skills, and Working Memory.

Space requirements: Change Three can be played in pairs or as a group. The easiest way to teach this game is to start with the group version. In the group version, students could remain in their seats facing one direction. In the pair version, depending on the classroom layout, students could stand in aisles between desks or desks could be moved to create a larger space to work in.

Teacher/Counselor participation: Coach.

In a large group: A student volunteers to be the Changer, and the rest of the group are Observers. The Changer stands where the Observers can see what the Changer is wearing, how hair is arranged, etc. The Changer turns slowly around so Observers can see all sides. They observe carefully until they think they are aware of everything about the Changer's appearance. The Changer then leaves the room and changes three things. Objects could be taken off or re-arranged.

Helpful Hint: It can be helpful to have the Coach or an aide accompany the Changer to help with the change.

When the Changer reenters the room, the Observers decide what is different. Observers can write down their ideas and then share their answers, or they can raise their hand and say what they think has changed. When all three changes have been identified, another student becomes the Changer. If students enjoy this experiment, it can be played many times, and after a while, they can be challenged to identify four, five, or six changes.

Played in pairs: Both players look carefully at what the other is wearing, how hair is arranged, etc. When both think they can remember their partner's physical appearance, they turn their backs to each other and change three things. Objects could be taken off or re-arranged. They have to turn back to each other at the same time. You could have them say:

ONE: "Ready?"
TWO: "Ready!"
BOTH: "One-two-three-turn!"

When they turn around, they decide what their partner changed.

Shape Copying (Delgado, 1986)

Goals addressed: Attention, Body Control, Observation, and Working Memory.

Space requirements: Open space, with students in a circle standing or sitting.

Teacher/Counselor participation: Participant and Coach.

One player goes to the center of the circle and takes an interesting body position. Another player volunteers to reproduce the position. It is important for the Observing Player to take time to look 360 degrees around the Posing Player to see each tiny detail. If the Leader can take 2-3 photos of the pose with a cellphone, there will be a record to refer back to. The Poser comes out of the pose, and the Observer takes the pose. Other players decide if the pose is exactly like the one made or if the Observer needs to make an adjustment.

Elephant and Giraffe (Aycox, 1997)

Goals addressed: Attention, Attention Shifting, Teamwork, and Working Memory.

Space requirements: Group stands in a circle with one player in the middle.

Teacher/Counselor participation: Player and Coach.

This is a team building/working memory game for young groups or groups that have great difficulty with working memory. The Center Player points to a player in the circle and calls out either Giraffe or Elephant, then counts to five as quickly as possible. For Giraffe, the player pointed to raises arms straight up in the air as if making the neck of a giraffe. For Elephant, the player pointed to becomes the trunk of the elephant and the players on either side create the ears. The player(s) must get into the position called in five seconds or whoever is most incorrect must replace the Center Player.

For a more complex version of this game, see 1776 in Chapter Three.

Sushi

Goals addressed: Attention, Attention Shifting, Following Directions, Listening, and Working Memory.

Space requirements: Students could stand at their desks or could be standing in a circle.

Teacher/Counselor participation: Leader

1. Start by teaching the first word and action,
2. then add the next word and action and practice in a random pattern,

3. then add the third word and action and practice with all three in a random pattern,

4. then add the fourth word and action and practice with all in a random pattern, and

5. finally add the fifth word and action and practice all in a random pattern.

When I say, "One" – Clap.

When I say, "Two" – Say, "Sushi."

When I say "Three" – Say "Waffle" and reach up with one arm.

When I say, "Four" – Point to the door.

When I say, "Five" – It's show time [Students make jazz hands – open both hands wide, hold them up by their faces, facing out, and wiggle them.]

People-Shelter-Storm

Goals addressed: Attention, Attention Shifting, Following Directions, Listening, Sequencing, Teamwork and Working Memory.

Space requirements: A large open space.

Teacher/Counselor participation: Leader.

Number of players: Must be divisible by three.

Divide students into groups of three. In each small group, two players create a shelter (roof) over the third player who is the Person. The Shelters stand facing each other and reach out their arms until their fingertips touch over the head of the Person.

When the Leader says, "People," the People leave their Shelters and find a new Shelter. The Shelters do not move. When the Leader says, "Shelter," the students creating the Shelters break apart and find a new Person to make a shelter around. In this instance, the People do not move. The Shelters can stay together or split up and join with different Shelters. When the Leader says, "Storm," everyone runs around for five seconds, and when the Leader says, "Time's up," they have to form into new groups of three. Shelter players can become People, and People can become Shelters, or they can keep the same part they had. However, players need to be flexible and take on whatever role is needed in their new small group.

Add On Memory Games

Goals addressed: Attention, Cognitive Flexibility, Sequencing, and Working Memory.

Space requirements: Open space with players in a circle.

Teacher/Counselor participation: Player.

This is any kind of game that starts with one player in the circle naming an item. The next player says the first item and adds one of their own, and so on around the circle. Each time another item is added, all the items must be said in order from the first to current one. The items could be the names of players, names of candy bars, food eaten at a picnic, things you would pack for a trip, etc.

Easiest version: For groups that have sequencing or working memory problems, the easiest way to practice this is every time a name or item is added to the series by a new person, go back to the first person in the circle and have each person repeat their own contribution in sequence until the last item added is reached. In other words, the repetition is done by the people whose contribution it actually was. In terms of sequencing, the players only need to remember who spoke before them. This is easy if the group is sitting in a circle and going around in order.

A more challenging version: To begin to challenge sequencing abilities, each student needs to remember everything in order themselves.

A little bit more challenging version: Instead of going around the circle in order, play popcorn style.

Only move to a more difficult version when you believe students are ready for the challenge.

Chosen (Aycox, 1997)

Goals addressed: Observation Skills, Problem solving, and Working Memory

Space requirements: This could be done with students sitting at their desks or sitting in chairs in a large circle.

Teacher/Counselor participation: Leader and Player.

The Leader starts as It in order to teach the game. Think of one thing that certain Players in the class/circle have in common and ask all of those Players to stand up by name. (For instance, they all could be wearing glasses or the same color of clothing or they all could be students who bring their lunch every day.) The Seated Players have to guess what the Standing Players have in common. When the correct commonality is guessed, another It can be chosen.

Helpful Hint: It may be helpful for the first few players who are It to confer with the Leader about what commonality to choose to make sure they really understand how to play the game. If they forget a student who does have that commonality, the Leader can help by suggesting that the forgotten student also stand up.

Variation: Instead of using people, the Leader could collect a group of objects that have something in common with each other.

Attention

Attention involves two aspects: Paying attention and sustaining attention. There are many reasons for this. A task or object may not grab a student's attention because too many other things are competing for their attention. Another reason could be the task/object itself is not being presented in an interestingly enough manner to attract them, or the task/object is just plain boring no matter how it is presented.

Other times the weakness lies in students' attenuation abilities. Attention might not be able to be sustained if the student is not motivated to pay attention to the task or if there is something else (noise, a smell, or a cell phone) in the environment that is distracting them. Students who have attention deficit hyperactivity disorder (ADHD) or who have experienced trauma may have difficulty sustaining attention. To know how to address the difficulty, it is important to understand the cause. A change of seat in the room away from a noisy radiator or a distracting desk neighbor may make a big difference. If not, the search for a cause can continue. In any case, attention can be improved through practice.

Here are some drama games that could assist in the development of attention:

Yes-No-You

Goals addressed: Attention, Attention Shifting, Body Control, Eye Contact, Sequencing, and Social Connection.

Space requirements: Large enough space for a circle.

Teacher/Counselor participation: Player.

Players stand in a circle. There are three types of movement-word pairs each player can make:

1. A player can turn to the player on the right, make eye contact, and gesture toward them with an open hand, and say, "Yes."

2. A player can turn to the player on the left, make eye contact, and gesture toward them with an open hand, and say, "No."

3. A player can make eye contact with any other player in the circle, gesture with an open hand to that player, and say, "You."

The best way to teach this game is first to teach and practice the movements for "Yes" all the way around the circle. Then practice the movements for "No" all the way around the circle. Then practice changing the direction of the movement between "Yes" and "No." The word and direction of the gesture can change depending on the choice of the player who received the most recent gesture.

Once everyone feels comfortable with the directions each word is said in and are remembering to gesture and make eye contact, add the third word and movement. The game continues with the three choices of direction. A lot of attention is needed to make the correct gesture in the correct direction, see when someone is pointing at them across the circle, and switch attention when the direction changes.

Yes-No-You is similar to Zip-Zap-Zop, which will be described later.

Mirroring (Spolin, 1963)

Goals addressed: Attention, Body Control, Eye Contact, Non-Verbal Communication, Observation Skills, Sensory Integration/Awareness, Social Connection, and Teamwork.

Space requirements: Open space where pairs can stand facing each other and move without touching another pair.

Teacher/Counselor participation: Coach.

Number of players: The group needs to be even in number to create pairs. If there is an odd number, create one "three-way mirror" (as in a department store). Put students with strongest attention skills in this group in the "three-way mirror," because it is not as easy as one-on-one.

Divide into pairs. Pairs face each other. One player will be the Leader who is looking into a mirror and taking the responsibility for moving. The other will be the Mirror and will copy whatever action the Leader takes.

Helpful Hint: One key to being able to follow the Leader is to make eye contact and watch the rest of the Leader's body out of peripheral vision. The other key is for the Leader to move very slowly. Tell players that the point of the activity is not to trick their partner, but to trick *you* so you cannot tell who is leading and who is following.

After the first partner has led for two-three minutes, stop, and have the pairs switch roles so that the Mirror can become the Leader, and the Leader can become the Mirror.

If your class is small enough or has the patience to listen to each other, you can check in with each pair after each round, asking about their experience. If you do this, you will want all pairs to listen to each other as different pairs may have had different experiences. At the end, you could ask who preferred being a leader versus being a follower.

Another variation that can be added if students have the attention skills: Start a round where one student is the Leader, but the Mirror can take over the leadership at will. When that happens, the Leader must become the Mirror. The leadership can pass back and forth between the two as many times as they want. One outcome of this can be that they lose awareness of who is leading and who is following. That can lead to great discussions about teamwork. What happens when two people are working together and learn how to give and take with each other? What happens when they do not give and take?

Follow The Leader (Boal, 1992)

Goals addressed: Attention, Body Control, Boundaries, and Teamwork.

Space requirements: Open space where students can move.

Teacher/Counselor participation: Coach.

The group divides into pairs. In each pair, one player volunteers to be the Leader and the other volunteers to be the Shadow. The Leader moves around the room slowly and the Shadow tries to follow and copy all their movements (or at least what can be seen from behind). This game is similar to Mirroring, although the players do not stay in one place, but move around the room. Part of the challenge for the Shadow is to stay the same amount of space behind the Leader all the time. This also means paying enough attention to sense when the Leader is going to stop, so as not to bump into the Leader. After one round, reverse roles.

Magical Power (Boal, 1992)

Goals addressed: Attention, Body Control, Boundaries, and Teamwork.
  Space requirements: Open space where students can move.
  Teacher/Counselor participation: Coach.
  The group divides into pairs. In each pair, one player volunteers to be the Magician and the other volunteers to be the Enchanted One. The Magician has magical powers in the palm of one of their hands (Players usually choose their dominant hand). The Enchanted One must follow where the palm of the hand designates, focusing on the palm and moving with it. If it comes toward the Enchanted One, the Enchanted One backs up. If it is moves away from the Enchanted One, the Enchanted One follows. If the palm moves up, so does the Enchanted One, etc. The Magician and the Enchanted One need to try to keep the same distance between the hand and the Enchanted One. After one round, reverse roles. It should look almost as if there is a force field magnetically controlling the movement.

In Plain View (Aycox, 1997)

Goals addressed: Attention, Inhibition, Observation Skills.
  Space requirements: Students could be at their desks.
  Teacher/Counselor participation: Leader and Coach.
  The Leader asks everyone to close their eyes while a small object is placed somewhere in plain sight in the classroom. It should not be hidden. Once it is in place, and the Leader is back where he/she started, players can open their eyes. Tell them what the object is and allow them first to look around from their desks. If no one can find it, allow several students to walk around the room and look. If they find it, they should not say where it is, but walk back to their desk and sit down. Allow everyone to get up and look (if they say they have already found it, they do not have to get up). When everyone has had a chance to find it, ask, "Where is it?"
  For the next round a new person can place a different object in plain sight while everyone closes their eyes.

Who's The Leader? (Spolin, 1963)

Goals addressed: Attention, Observation Skills, Problem-solving, Sensory Integration, and Teamwork.

Space requirements: Open space where class can sit in a circle on the floor or in chairs.

Teacher/Counselor participation: Player and Coach.

All players sit in a circle, except for one Detective, who leaves the room. While the Detective is gone, the Coach decides on one player who will be the Leader. The Leader begins a rhythmic movement, and the rest of the players copy it. The Leader can change the rhythmic movement at random, and the group tries to change their movement at the same time.

The Detective is called back into the room and observes the group to decide who the Leader is. The Detective can stand inside or outside of the circle, using sight and sound cues for clues. From time to time the Leader *must* change the movement, and all the rest of the players must try to change as quickly and unnoticeably as possible. The Detective is given a certain number of guesses, usually three. If the Detective guesses correctly, a new Detective is chosen and the old one can rejoin the circle. After the new Detective leaves the room, the Coach chooses the new Leader, and the next round game begins.

Helpful Hint: The followers need to avoid looking directly at the Leader because that will give the Leader away. This can be a difficult task for young players.

If the Detective cannot guess the Leader, there is no penalty. Give the Leader and the Detective applause and tell both, "Good job!"

Critical Thinking: Ask students what they did to fool the Detective. Ask the Detective what clues worked to identify who the Leader was. This helps all to understand what to observe for when they become the Detective.

Helpful Hint: When students are learning this game, it can be helpful to have two Detectives who can confer with each other about the clues they are seeing.

Dog And Bone

Goals addressed: Body Control, Impulse Control, Listening Skills, Sensory Integration, and Teamwork.

Space requirements: Large open space.

Teacher/Counselor participation: Coach.

Supplies needed: Blindfold, A Mat for the Dog, Rawhide Bone or Paper Towel Roll to represent the bone, Masking tape for the starting line.

This game is enjoyed most by young children. One player volunteers to be the Dog, is blindfolded, and lies down on the mat with the "bone" in front of him/her at one end of the room. The rest of the group stands at a distance from the Dog on the starting line. The Dog must listen carefully while the rest of the group tries to sneak up to steal the bone. If the Dog hears any noise, he/she must point in the direction of the sound and bark. Whoever is caught must go back to the starting line. Whoever steals the bone gets to be the next Dog.

Eventually the players may realize that they can work together as a team to distract the dog and allow one of them to get the bone. Let them figure this out on their own.

Helpful Hint: This game is competitive, pitting the group against one player. Only play this if your group can handle winning and losing.

Helpful Hint: It can be a good idea to have a different blindfold for each Dog so germs are not passed around.

Variation: The Queen/King Has A Headache!

Goals addressed: Body Control, Impulse Control, Listening Skills, Sensory Integration, and Teamwork.

Space requirements: Large open space.

Teacher/Counselor participation: Coach.

Supplies needed: Blindfolds, Chair for Throne, Crown and Masking Tape for the starting line.

Younger and older students enjoy this game. The Queen or King of the Kingdom has a headache and, therefore, does not want to hear any noise because it makes their head hurt more. The Queen or King is blindfolded and sits on a throne at one end of the room. The group tries to sneak up on the Queen or King, and if he/she hears any noise, he/she points in that direction and moans loudly. Whoever is caught needs to go back to the starting line. The player who tags the King or Queen on the knee before getting caught becomes the next Queen or King.

Helpful Hint: This game is competitive, pitting the group against one player. Only play this if your group can handle winning and losing.

Critical thinking: Older students will be able to discuss ideas about this game. Ask the Queens and Kings if they were able to hear or sense in a different way with the blindfold on. Did their hearing improve? Were they able to hear directionally? Was it easy for players sneaking up on the monarchs to be quiet and control their bodies, or did they make more noise than they expected?

Helpful Hint: It can be a good idea to have a blindfold for each Queen/ King so germs are not passed around.

Attention Shifting

As mentioned above, difficulties with attention are often interwoven with attention shifting problems. Moving attention from one task to another requires two actions: Letting go of attention to the first while shifting and connecting to the second. Perhaps a student's attention is so strongly focused on the first task that they cannot let go of it. This can be a difficulty that students with autism (ASD) or ADHD struggle with. Another cause of not being able to shift attention may be that the new task is not interesting or unique enough to capture the student's attention. Other students have difficulty transitioning from the first to the second task, because their attention gets focused on a totally different task before they can re-attenuate on the second.

The drama games listed here work on improving attention shifting:

On The Bank/In The River

Goals addressed: Attention Shifting, Body Control, Boundaries, Inhibition/ Impulse Control, and Listening.

Space required: A long thin space at least eight feet wide.

Teacher/Counselor participation: Leader.

Supplies needed: Masking tape.

This is a wonderful quick warm-up game and gets players energized.

Create a line on the floor with masking tape. On one side is the bank and on the other side is the river. Everyone starts on the same side. The Leader calls out "On the bank," or "In the river," and Players hop to the correct side. The Leader can try to trick players by repeating a command more than once.

Elimination: The group can play the elimination version of the game: If a player makes a mistake, they are eliminated. The only problem with that is the eliminated players do not get warmed up as well as the players who stay in the game longer.

Zip-Zap-Zop

Goals addressed: Attention, Attention Shifting, Sequencing, and Social Connections.

Space requirements: Large enough for a circle.

Teacher/Counselor participation: Player.

The group stands in a circle, facing inward. Player A starts by looking and pointing at someone else in the circle (Player B) and saying, "Zip!" Player B looks and points at someone else (Player C) and says, "Zap!" Player C looks and points at a fourth player (Player D) and says, "Zop!" Player D starts at "Zip" and points to someone else, and the game continues. The Zips, Zaps, and Zops are popcorned around the circle with no specific pattern created. However, Zip, Zap, and Zop must be remembered in sequence.

This game is similar to Yes-No-You. It is a great group energizer.

Dude!

Goals addressed: Attention, Eye Contact, Initiation, Non-Verbal Communication, and Verbal Expressiveness.

Space Requirements: Large enough space for a circle.

Teacher/Counselor participation: Player.

The group stands in a circle facing in. Everyone looks down. At various points, each person looks up, and if they catch the eye of another person, they both say, "Dude!" to each other and change places in the circle. After they have moved, they look down again.

Helpful Hint: If students are not looking up, the Leader must step in and say, "Look up!" or "Look down!" to ensure that everyone is playing.

Helpful Hint: Encourage players to use different tones of voice when they say "Dude!" to create the very beginning of characters and a relationship between the characters.

Pass The Sound/Pass The Movement I

Goals addressed: Attention, Attention Shifting, Body Control, and Sensory Integration & Awareness.

Space requirements: Large enough space for a circle.

Teacher/Counselor participation: Player.

The group stands in a circle facing in. The beginning player passes a sound and a movement to the player on their left or right. That player copies the sound and movement back to the first, turns, and passes the same sound and movement on to the player on the other side. When the sound and movement gets all the way around the circle, the next player creates a new sound and movement to pass. This can continue until everyone has a chance to initiate a new sound and movement.

Advanced Variation: Pass The Sound/Pass The Movement II

Goals addressed: Attention, Attention Shifting, Body Control, and Sensory Integration & Awareness.

Space requirements: Large enough space for a circle.

Teacher/Counselor participation: Player.

The group stands in a circle facing in. The beginning player passes a sound and a movement to the player on the left or right. That player copies the movement back to the first, turns, and transforms it into a *new* sound and movement that is passed to the next player in the circle. The sound and movement is mirrored and then changed all the way around the circle. The game continues without stopping around the circle as many times as players want to play.

Three Ball Pass

Goals addressed: Attention, Attention Shifting, Teamwork, and Working Memory.

Space requirements: Large enough for a circle.

Teacher/Counselor participation: Player and Leader.

Supplies needed: A ball that bounces, a ball that does not bounce (like a beach ball), and a small, light ball that fits in the hand and is easy to grasp (a whiffle ball or koosh ball works well).

The Leader gets another person's attention by calling out their name and bouncing a ball to them. That player does the same to another player. This continues for a while. Then the Leader adds a second ball that can only be thrown. The name of the person to whom it will be tossed is called to get that person's attention before the ball is thrown. Both balls are passed at the same time, with attention paid to avoid both balls being thrown to the same player simultaneously. After a while, the Leader adds a third ball. This ball is passed to the person on the left or right. Again, that person's attention is alerted by saying their name before being given the ball. The direction of the third ball can change.

This game can be over-stimulating for students with ADHD; however, their focus and attention skills can be increased over time by playing the game with one ball until all the students are able to pay attention and shift attention well. Then play with two balls until they can handle that well, before trying to play with three balls.

Pattern Ball Passing

Goals addressed: Attention, Sequencing, Rhythm, Teamwork, and Working Memory.

Space requirements: Large enough for a small circle.

Teacher/Counselor participation: Player, unless several groups are playing, then serves as a Coach to all the groups.

Number of players: This game works best with between four and eight players in a group.

Supplies needed: Several balls of different colors and/or sizes that can be easily tossed and caught.

The group stands in a circle. One player starts the first ball around the circle in a pattern in which every player receives the ball once. Then the ball is thrown back to the first player. The group practices this pattern a number of times until they can remember it. Then a second player takes a different colored ball and creates a new pattern with that ball. Again, every player receives the ball once, and it is returned to the player who started the pattern. The group practices this second pattern until they can remember it. Then the group attempts to do both patterns simultaneously. As working memory and sequencing skills improve, the group can add balls and practice new patterns until everyone in the circle is starting a ball.

Sequencing

The ability to arrange and remember items or tasks into a specific order is sequencing. The order can be arbitrary, based on logic, or based on nature.

For instance, the alphabet is an arbitrary sequence. The game Zip-Zap-Zop has an arbitrary sequence. Numbers have a logical sequence, as do mathematical formulas. A 24-hour period follows the same sequence every day of the year. Stories always follow the sequence of beginning, middle, and end. Most projects in which something is put together usually must be done in sequence, or the item will not end up finished correctly.

Students who have sequencing difficulties usually get directions out of order. This creates problems in spelling, math, history, and just about every task one is asked to complete in life from getting dressed to driving. Learning sequences requires multiple repetitions. The more difficulties one has with sequencing, the more repetitions have to be done. Certain drama games can help students practice sequencing.

Hand Squeeze (Pass the Pulse)

Goals addressed: Boundaries, Sensory Integration & Awareness, and Sequencing.

Space requirements: Enough space for group to stand or sit in a circle and hold hands.

Teacher/Counselor participation: Player.

Everyone gets into a circle and holds hands. A volunteer passes a hand squeeze in one direction around the circle. After a recipient receives a squeeze from one side, the squeeze is passed to the hand of the person on the other side. Eventually, the squeeze returns to the first person. If the squeeze gets lost, the group can start again.

Hand-Squeeze Variation: The squeeze can be passed around the circle at varying speeds.

Hand-Squeeze Variation: Arms can be crossed in front of the body so each player's left hand is holding the right hand of the person on their right and vice versa.

Hand-Squeeze Variation: The squeeze can be passed in both directions simultaneously.

Fortunately-Unfortunately

Goals addressed: Attention Skills, Cognitive Flexibility, Decision-making, Generating Alternatives, Listening Skills, Problem-solving, Reframing, Sequencing, Teamwork, Verbal Communication, and Working Memory.

Space requirements: This can be done at students' desks, but the sequencing is sometimes clearer when the group is sitting or standing in a circle.

Teacher/Counselor participation: Player and Coach.

The group builds a story taking turns. The First Storyteller starts the story. After setting the scene and introducing the main character(s) in a few sentences, the First Storyteller pauses and the Second Storyteller takes over. The Second Storyteller and starts with "Unfortunately … " and explains an obstacle that blocks the main character(s) from their task. Once the obstacle or problem has been introduced, the Third Storyteller takes over and starts with "Fortunately …" and explains how the main character(s) removes the obstacle. The story alternates between Fortunately and Unfortunately around the circle until the story ends (Always end on a Fortunately!)

Helpful Hint: If a storyteller forgets what has happened to get the story to its current point, the Leader and/or other players can remind the current storyteller what has happened so far.

Labor Dance

Goals addressed: Body Control, Gross Motor Skills, Rhythm, Sequencing, Teamwork, and Working Memory.

Space requirements: Open space where students can move.

Teacher/Counselor participation: Coach.

Supplied required: Occupations on slips of paper in a box.

Divide the class into smaller groups of three or four Players. Each group agrees on a different occupation (or the Coach can have a box of occupations so each group can choose one). The small group acts out/pantomimes activities that people would do in the course of that job.

Then the Coach tells each group to create a dance from one or more of those actions. If the group has difficulty with this, suggest they use the rhythm of the actions for the basis of the dance. Dances have a sequence or pattern of movement: Perhaps ABAB or ABCABC. Keep it simple at first.

When the groups are ready, have each of them show their dance to the rest of the class. After everyone has seen the dance, each group can teach their dance to the class.

See if all the sequences can be put together into one dance. For young Players, the Coach may need to facilitate this. Older groups that have developed flexibility and teamwork may be able to do this together.

Helpful Hint: Having a variety of instrumental music at hand that have different tempos would be useful to help students with creating an order for the dance's sequencing.

Variations: Animal Dance, Machine Dance, Weather Dance or Season Dance: Instead of occupations, small groups could pick an animal and explore the movements each animal makes or a household machine, types of weather, or activities done in different seasons.

Chain Pantomime (Aycox, 1997)

Goals addressed: Attention, Observation Skills, Sequencing, and Working Memory.

Space requirements: Enough space so that at least two players can pantomime and be seen by everyone in the room. This may mean creating an Acting/Audience area.

Teacher/Counselor participation: Coach.

Four Players leave the room and decide on an order they will come back in. While they are out in the hall, the class decides on a specific series of actions that complete a task that one Player can perform. It could be anything from getting on a bus (waiting, climbing up the steps, paying the fare, and finding a seat) to saddling a horse. A volunteer agrees to pantomime the action (no sound). The volunteer might want to practice once before the first Player returns so the sequence of the actions is set.

Player #1 enters the room and is instructed to watch the Volunteer Actor closely as the task is pantomimed. No guesses as to what is being done are to be made. Afterwards, the Volunteer Actor sits down. Actor #1 gets Player #2 to come in. Player #1 acts out what he/she saw, while Player #2 watches closely. Then Player #1 leaves and sends in Player #3. Player #3 watches Player #2 act out what he/she saw. Then Player #2 leaves and sends Player #4 in. Player #4 watches Player #3 act out the pantomime. At the end of the pantomime, Player #3 goes back out into the hallway.

Player #4 gets three guesses as to what Player #3 pantomimed. Player #3 comes back in and has three guesses what Player #2 was pantomiming. Player #2 comes in and guesses what Player #1 was pantomiming. Player #1 comes in and guesses what the Volunteer Actor was pantomiming.

If everyone is correct, everyone did excellent observing and sequencing. If the pantomime changed, then either the observation or the acting was not as clear as it could have been, or the sequencing of the actions were off.

If no one guessed the pantomime correctly, have the Volunteer Actor act it out again and see if the four Players can guess what is being done.

Variation: Pantomime Down the Line

This version gets everyone involved. Divide the group into three to five smaller groups of the same number. Each small group lines up facing the same direction. The Leader shows the last person in each line a word or a picture of what they are to pantomime (everyone will be acting out the same thing) and tells them if it is a noun or verb (object or action). The last people get back in their line.

When the Leader says, "Go," the last person taps the person in front of him/her on the back. That person turns around and watches the last person in line pantomime out the object or action.

When the next-to-last person thinks they know what it is, they turn back around and tap the shoulder of the person in front of them. In this way, the action or object is "passed down the line."

Whichever line gets the correct answer first, gets a point (or if competition is not appropriate for this class, they get the applause).

Helpful Hint: The Coach moves from the back of the lines to the front. As each pantomime arrives at the first person in line and they turn back around, they can write on a piece of paper what they think they received or they can whisper the word to the Coach. Once all the lines have finished, each first person in the line reveals what they received.

Magic Dollar Bill Trick (Spencer)

Goals addressed: Attention, Fine Motor Skills, Sequencing, and Working Memory.

Space requirements: This activity could be taught with students at their desks.

Teacher/Counselor participation: Coach.

Supplies needed: One dollar bill (or piece of paper in a rectangular shape and size of a dollar bill) and two large paperclips for each student.

With George Washington facing the Magician, bend the right side of the dollar bill toward the center far enough to cover George Washington's face. Place a paperclip on the top edge of the bill over the number one where it is covering Washington's face.

Bend the remaining left side of the bill behind to the back of the bill. It should be the same length as the bend in the front. [If you look at the bill from the top, the folds will make an S shape.] Place the second paperclip on the top edge of the bill over the number one to hold that fold in place. Only clip the front flap (now in back) and the center of the bill. In other words, the paperclip will not cover all three pieces paper created by the folds, just the two rear pieces.

Warning: Don't make a crease or flatten the folds in the bill. The "folded" areas should be open: More like a tunnel.

Now for the magic: Hold the two side edges of the bill, pull out firmly and quickly. The paperclips will fly off the dollar bill and into the air. When they come down, they will be hooked together!

If you want to see the trick in action, see the amazing Kevin Spencer do it at https://hocusfocusmagicclub.com/lesson-4-linking-paper-clips/

Emotional Regulation

As mentioned above, emotional regulation is the ability to recognize emotions in oneself and others and the control to choose how and when to express them. No emotion is inherently bad or good. All serve the function of sending a message to the person about what is going on around them.

For instance, anger is a very powerful emotion. Typically, it is a response to a threat of some kind. It releases adrenalin into the body so the person has the energy to confront or attack the threat or to change the situation (Bilodeau, 1992; Goleman, 2005; Tavris, 1989). Without anger, we would allow others to invade our personal boundaries and damage our lives. We would never recognize social injustice and try to stop it. However, not everyone knows how to listen to the messages that anger sends.

A healthy way to regulate anger is to stop, recognize it, evaluate the situation, and make the best choice to change the situation. That could be attacking someone physically or verbally, but more often it involves a more carefully thought out constructive solution. A thought out, appropriate response to anger would be considered an emotionally intelligent one (Goleman, 2005).

Developmentally, the ability to regulate emotions develops over time as we grow. It depends on seeing good role models in action from an early age. Before we can do anything with our emotions, we must identify them. Emotions are usually experienced and expressed physically, so a good place to start recognizing and identifying emotions is with our own bodies.

Recognizing Emotions in Self

Students who do not understand what they are feeling are not going to be able to talk about what is going on with them. They will respond to the question, "What are you feeling right now?" with "I don't know." More often than not, they are not avoiding the question; they really do not know. They may feel a rush of energy inside, but have no words for labeling it.

To recognize emotions in oneself requires awareness of the physical feelings and the interior thoughts that occur in tandem in a situation. This means that one of the first places to start is identifying how the emotion is physicalized and what that posture, tension, and movement feels like. Then start listening for the thoughts you are thinking or looking at the components of the situation.

Confusion sometimes occurs in this process because many emotions are caused by the release of the same hormones, and the body responds with similar physical reactions. For instance, anger, excitement, love, and fear are all caused by a rush of adrenalin. This increases the heart rate, constricts the blood vessels, and opens the airways so more oxygen can come into the lungs. We experience our hearts pounding, become very alert, feel hot, turn red in the face, and begin to hyperventilate. What we are doing or thinking in the situation often determines which emotion we feel. For instance, if you are threatened by someone who is your equal, you may think, "How dare he say that to me?" and get angry. If you are threatened by someone who has authority over you or who is intimidating, you may think, "I'm going to be in so much trouble – I'm doomed!" and feel fear. But if you have just kissed a guy or girl you are very attracted to, you may be falling in love!

A beautiful example of how thinking about an event differently can change what feeling is evoked is in the movie *Parenthood*. Steve Martin's character, an extremely anxious person, feels like a failure as a father. Toward the end of the film, in response to his worries, Grandma tells him a story:

> You know, when I was 19, Grandpa took me on a roller coaster. Up-down-up-down.
>
> What a ride! It was so interesting to me that a ride could make me so frightened, so scared, so sick, and so thrilled all together. Some didn't like it. They went on the merry-go-round. That just goes around. Nothing. I like the roller coaster. You get more out of it!

In the following scene, Steve and his wife are watching their daughter perform in the school play, when their youngest child, thinking his sister is being bullied by one of the other characters, runs up on stage to save her. Chaos ensues. The audience of parents is aghast! The play is being ruined! Steve Martin is on the verge of total humiliation. He glances over at his wife, and she is laughing! Suddenly he hears a roller coaster in his imagination (we hear it, too!) and realizes that what's happening isn't a tragedy – it's hysterically funny! It all depends on your attitude toward it. He makes a choice to interpret his experience differently and starts to smile, and then laugh. It is a turning point for his character (Howard, 1989).

Emotion Walks

Goals addressed: Body Control, Emotional Expression, Emotional Identification, Inhibition, and Non-Verbal Expression.

Space requirements: Large space in which group can move around without bumping into each other.

Teacher/Counselor participation: Leader.

Players walk around the room expressing an emotion the Leader has called out. When the Leader calls out, "Freeze," the players freeze in a position that expresses that emotion. Then the Leader calls out a different emotion, the players unfreeze and begin walking around expressing that emotion.

If players get very wound up playing this game, the Leader can alternate walking with an emotion and walking in a neutral or calm state. That builds more emotional regulation into the game.

Derole after this experiment.

Pass The Face

Goals addressed: Emotional Expression, Emotion Identification, Emotional Intensity Identification, and Non-verbal Communication.

Space requirements: Large enough space for students to sit in a circle.

Teacher/Counselor participation: Leader and Player.

The group sits in a circle facing in. One player makes a face and turns to look at the player on their right or left. That player copies the first player's face and turns to pass it to the next player in the circle. After the face makes it all the way around the circle, the Leader asks what emotion was passed and why the group thinks it was that emotion. Then another player can create a face and pass it. Usually everyone wants a turn to create a face.

Variation: Pass The Face Reactions

Goals addressed: Empathy, Emotion Expression, Emotion Identification, Emotional Intensity Identification, and Non-verbal Communication.

Space requirements: Large enough space for students to sit in a circle.
Teacher/Counselor participation: Leader and Player.

The group sits in a circle. One player makes a face and turns to look at the player on the right or left. That player reacts facially to the emotion on the face and passes the reaction to the next player. Reactions continue being passed around the circle. The reactions can continue to be passed around the circle, or the Leader can stop the reaction when it gets back to the first player. Discuss what emotion players received and what their emotional reaction was. Ask if the player who received the reaction perceived it as the emotion identified by the passer or if they thought it was a different emotion.

Emotion Orchestra/Symphony

Goals addressed: Cognitive Empathy, Emotional Expression, Emotional Identification, Emotional Intensity Identification, Impulse Control, and Teamwork.

Space requirements: A space large enough for students to gather together in a group as if they are an orchestra. They need enough space to move their arms and upper bodies without hitting anyone near them.

Teacher/Counselor participation: Conductor.

Each player chooses an emotion and creates a sound or a series of sounds that express it. Players making similar emotions/sounds find each other so there is a section for each emotion, just as an orchestra has a section for strings, woodwinds, percussion, and brass instruments. The Leader or a player serves as the Conductor and signals the Emotion Orchestra to begin. When the Conductor points to a section, they make their sounds. If the Conductor's hands are raised, the players become louder and more intense. If the Conductor's hands are lowered, the players become softer. The Conductor can silence an emotion section or the whole orchestra by making an agreed upon gesture for silence. Emotion sections can play individually or together in different combinations decided on by the Conductor.

Variation: Emotional Orchestra With Words

Goals addressed: Cognitive Empathy, Emotional Expression, Emotional Identification, Emotional Intensity Identification, and Teamwork.

Space requirements: Same as for Emotional Orchestra with Sounds.

Teacher/Counselor participation: Leader and Conductor.

Each player chooses an emotion and decides on either one word or phrase to express it. Players making similar emotions find each other so there is a section for each emotion represented. The conductor conducts in the same way as for Emotional Orchestra.

Recognizing Emotions in Others

To recognize emotions in others, students have to learn to recognize what the emotion looks like on the other person's face and body and what it sounds like in their voice. This can be difficult for students who have ASD and ADHD. Many of the drama games below allow students to experiment with what the physical expressions of different emotions look like and the changes in emotion that come with different intensities. Obviously, there will be a difference between what a person looks like if they are a little sad or very depressed. Discussions also need to happen about how some people express emotions differently than others. For instance, sometimes people who are afraid to get angry, laugh. Sometimes people have learned not to show any outward emotion. When this happens, or whenever one is confused about what another is feeling, it is OK to ask, "What are you feeling?" instead of guessing.

Group Mood

Goals addressed: Cognitive Empathy, Emotional Expression, Emotional Identification, Emotional Intensity Identification, and Non-verbal Communication

Space requirements: Students could be at their desks, but it would be better if they could get up and move around the room.

Teacher/Counselor participation: Coach.

One player leaves the room. While the player is gone, the rest of the group decides on an emotion that they all will portray. They do not have to copy each other. They are free to express the emotion in different ways and at different intensities. On return, the player must identify what emotion the group is portraying.

Making An Entrance

Goals addressed: Cognitive Empathy, Emotional Expression, Emotion Identification, Emotional Intensity Identification, and Nonverbal Communication.

Space requirements: Students could be sitting at their desks as long as everyone has a clear view of the door.

Teacher/Counselor participation: Coach.

Explain that when actors come onstage, they must already be expressing what the character is feeling. One player leaves the room with the Coach or an assistant. Together they decide on an emotion the player will portray when entering the room. The player "makes an entrance," non-verbally showing the emotion. The group guesses what emotion is being portrayed.

This game is the opposite of Group Mood. In Group Mood no one is put on the spot to perform alone. Making an Entrance is a more advanced activity for when students feel more confident performing alone.

Helpful Hint: A set of index cards could be made that list a variety of emotions, and the person going out to Make an Entrance could pick a card to choose their emotion. If students are young, keep the emotions simple and easily actable. As students gain more experience, more subtle intensities of emotions can be added to the pack.

Emotional Greetings

Goals addressed: Emotional Expression, Emotional Identification, Non-Verbal Expression, and Verbal Expression.

Space requirements: Large open space where students can move freely.

Teacher/Counselor participation: Leader.

Number of players: The group needs to work in pairs, so there needs to be an even number of players, or the Leader needs to become a partner.

Participants find a partner and stand back to back. Each round the Leader calls out a different emotion. The participants turn to face each other and greet each other with that emotion. The partners can stay with each other for the whole game, or they can change partners each round.

Sculpting Emotions

Goals addressed: Body Awareness, Cognitive Empathy, Emotional Expression, Emotional Identification, Emotional Intensity Identification, Non-Verbal Expression, and Teamwork.

Space requirements: Open space in which students can work in pairs.

Teacher/Counselor participation: Leader.

The drama game of sculpting helps players embody an idea or concept. One player poses another player to physically create an individual statue or poses several players to create a group statue. The player who is the Sculptor should first ask the player who is serving as the sculpture or clay if they are OK being touched. If they do not feel comfortable being touched (or if school rules prohibit touch), the Sculptor can show the player how to pose, and they can copy the position, gestures, and facial expression.

In pairs: One player volunteers to be the Sculptor, and the other is the Sculpture. Tell Sculptors to create a statue that expresses a specific emotion. Have everyone do the same emotion, but say that it could be any intensity of it. When all the Sculptures are done, the Sculptors can walk around the "Emotion Museum" they have created and look at all the versions of the emotion. Ask Sculptors to identify the common physical stances, facial expressions, gestures, or muscle tensions that depict that emotion. The intensity of each sculpt can be assessed. Then sculptors and sculpts can trade roles and sculpt a different emotion. After each round, be sure to have students "shake off the emotion," especially if it is one that is intense or uncomfortable.

Helpful Hint: Real emotions can be created when players are sculpted because the physical muscle tension, facial expression, breathing, and body posture can actually evoke the feeling of certain emotional experiences.[1] This is why de-roling after sculpting is so important.

Helpful Hint: Drama experiments need to be done in a nonjudgmental manner. There are certain times the Leader may need to allow gestures that are not considered polite but are gestures that do express the identified emotion. This will probably happen when you have students sculpt anger.

As the facilitator, you have a choice. When you announce the emotion, you can say, "I know there are rude gestures that express this emotion; please do not use them in your statues." Or you can allow students free reign and say, "I understand that many angry people use that gesture. Why do you think they do that? What do they want the other person to feel?" and turn the situation into a teachable moment on civility.

Helpful Hint: If a student creates a sculpture that does not express the emotion – either by being unexpressive or by expressing a different emotion, ask the student to make a change in their sculpture that would add one of the common physical aspects identified in the other sculptures. If your students are respectful of each other and serious about the game, you could ask them to help by each making one adjustment to the statue to make it a little bit more like the emotion.

Emotion Spectrogram

Goals addressed: Cognitive Empathy, Emotional Expression, Emotional Identification, and Emotional Intensity Identification.

Space requirements: Large space in which group can move around without bumping into each other.

Teacher/Counselor participation: Leader.

Supplies suggested: If needed, masking tape to mark the spectrum on the floor.

A spectrogram is an imaginary line in space that creates a continuum from low or zero to high or ten (or another number) on which players can evaluate how strongly they feel about a situation or criterion. It can be helpful to indicate the spectrogram on the floor when first teaching a group how to do it.

Create a spectrogram and assign one end as Low and the other as High. The leader explains this spectrogram is exploring the intensity of different emotions. Selected players take a position on the spectrogram and create a sculpture that expresses what the intensity of the emotion would be at that place on the spectrogram. After players have created their statues, the rest of the group, who have been observing, need to determine if the statues appropriately represent the order of the continuum or if they need to switch places. They can also determine if there is an intensity that is missing and can devise an appropriate sculpt for that spot.

Be sure to have students derole from the emotion they have sculpted.

Emotion Shifting

Emotions do not stay the same, they change from hour to hour and sometimes, even from minute to minute! Children often focus only on the emotion they are feeling at the moment and are not aware that by this afternoon or tomorrow morning, they may feel completely different. With all the depression and anxiety that has been reported at epidemic levels in all ages of school children, students need to understand that not only can an emotion passively change from time to time, but they have the capacity to make a choice to actively change it.

Observing Emotions On Video

Goals addressed: Cognitive Empathy, Emotional Identification, Emotional Intensity Identification, and Observation Skills.

Space requirements: Students can sit at their desks.

Teacher/Counselor participation: Leader.

Supplies required: Find several emotional scenes in movies or TV shows which are age-appropriate.

A few recommended movie scenes are:

Holes (Davis, 2003) **Scene 23**: One More Hole

My Dog Skip (Russell, 2000) **Scene 4**: Goodbye to Dink, **Scenes 5 and 6**: Birthday Party and Not Asking, **Scene 8**: Skip Driving.

Parenthood (Howard, 1989) **Scene 15**: The Birthday Party.

The Sandlot (Evans, 1993) **Scene 8**: The Thing Behind the Fence, **Scene 14**: The Hard Stuff, **Scene 16**: The Babe's Ball.

The Secret Garden (Holland, 1993) **Scene 15**: Sharing Secrets, **Scene 17**: Two People Afraid,

Maybe **Scene 19**: Letting in Light.

Wonder (Chboskey, 2017) **Scene 4**: (second half from dinner on). **Scene 7**: After school with friends.

Preview scenes before you show them so you know what the conflict in the scene is and whether it is age appropriate for your class.

Play students the video clips. You may need to play the clip twice: Once to get the gist of what is happening and who the characters are, and the second time to identify emotions. Ask them to identify what each character is feeling at the beginning, middle, and end of the scene. Does their emotion change or not? If it changes, why does it change? What happened to change it?

Often emotion identification relies on the situation. Watching a full scene can clarify what emotions are being presented and what creates emotional change.

I have not included the Pixar moving *Inside/Out* (Docter, 2015) in the list of movies to identify emotions from because a) observing cartoon characters is not the same as observing a real human face and b) each of the basic emotions are obvious. However, *Inside/Out* is a wonderful film to use to help students understand basic emotions and how they work inside us and affect our behavior.

Emotion Map

Goals addressed: Cognitive Empathy, Emotional Identification, Task organization.

Space requirements: Large space on the floor or across several tables so drawing can be done on large paper.

Teacher/Counselor participation: Leader.

Materials required: Long rolls of butcher paper, markers, tape or thumbtacks, and Post-it notes.

This exercise was first developed by Shakespeare and Company, a theatre in Connecticut, and was written about by Karen Bovard (2000) in *Teaching Tolerance,* a magazine for teachers published twice a year by the Southern Poverty Law Center. If you are interested in receiving *Teaching Tolerance,* you can subscribe for free at https://www.tolerance.org/

Brainstorm a list of common emotions. Then brainstorm a list of places/locations. Using the emotions, create metaphorical places/locations that could represent environments on an emotion map of the world. For example, your world could include a Volcano of Anger, the Clouds of Relaxation, the Moody Meadow, the Whirlpool of Fear, the Ferris Wheel of Fun, etc. Students can each pick a place they would like to draw on the map. If you have a class that likes to plan together and enjoys thinking metaphorically, the class could plan where each emotional place should be in relation to the others. If not, it is perfectly fine to have students draw wherever they choose on the paper.

When the emotional places are finished, give a tour of the map so everyone can see and appreciate everyone else's work. Put the map up on a wall in the classroom.

Each student can draw an icon or avatar on a Post-It Note and place it on the emotional space they are in currently. This map helps students (and the teacher or counselor) track the emotions and moods they are in throughout the day. It could be used to check in and check out of class each day. What students begin to learn from the emotion map is that emotions come and emotions go. They (and you) may discover patterns in their emotions. For instance, maybe every time a student comes in angry at the start of the day, they become depressed by the end of the day, or every time a student comes in sleepy, they get into a fight.

Something to consider: If the emotion map includes movable Post-It Notes, identities of students will not remain private and anonymous for long. Students will be able to see each other move their Post-Its around. Public admission of emotional states can make one vulnerable. A class of mature, sensitive students may start to reach out to support classmates who identify as sad or angry. However, if students in your class might use this personal information for bullying, I recommend making the map, discussing it, and putting it up on your wall, but not having students identify where they are on it.

To read the full article on the emotion map, go to http://www.tolerance.org/magazine/number-17-spring-2000/emotion-map

Grounding

Goals addressed: Shifting emotions and Stress Management.

Space requirements: This could be done sitting at a desk or standing up.

Teacher/Counselor participation: Leader.

The purpose of grounding is to bring students into the present moment and help them find a sense of safety within their bodies. Students stop and take a few slow deep breaths. Then, standing in that place, they look around and bring their attention in the space they are in to:

- Five objects they can see
- Four textures they can feel
- Three sounds they can hear

- Two odors they can smell
- One thing they can taste

The Leader should announce each of the five things to pay attention to, providing enough time for students to complete the task silently. Encourage them to use their imaginations and senses to really see, feel, hear, smell, and taste the items they have chosen.

This ability to re-create senses in the imagination is one that grows with practice. It was an exercise that Constantin Stanislavski (1948) used with his acting students to teach them how to fully inhabit the characters they would re-create onstage.

Grounding always pulls the person into the present moment. Because the person is focused on connecting with their senses, there is no room in their consciousness for out-of-control emotions.

Emotional Suppression

Emotional suppression can be positive or negative. If an emotion is valid and can be expressed in an effective and appropriate manner through words and other behavior, then it does not need to be suppressed; it can be expressed. However, if a person does not know how to express an emotion appropriately in the moment, it might be useful to know how to suppress it until such time as they understand the message their emotion is sending them and can choose an appropriate response. Sometimes people repress emotions unconsciously because they are afraid of that emotion or want to deny that it exists. The less one knows about emotions and how to work with them, the more often they will be repressed or suppressed instead of explored and understood.

Over the past ten years there have been many reports of children and teens in the U.S. struggling with tension, anxiety, trauma, and depression. (Marso, 2019). Statistics always run several years behind. The most current figures at the time of this writing are from 2017 when 3.2 million adolescents, ages 12-17, were diagnosed with major depression, up from 2 million in 2005 (Aspegren, 2020). National statistics on children with depression are difficult to find. The National Institute of Mental Health only lists statistics for adolescents and adults. Even more mental health issues have been suspected as arising in relation to the COVID-19 pandemic.

During depression and other mental illnesses, when students become dysregulated, their sympathetic nervous system has gone into overdrive. Breathing, getting more oxygen into the body and cleaning out the carbon dioxide built up in the muscles, helps start up the parasympathetic nervous system, which calms the body down. Many simple breathing exercises can help students calm down from intense emotions.

Diaphragmatic Breathing

Goals addressed: Emotional Release, Stress Management, and Relaxation.
    Space requirements: Students can do this anywhere.
    Teacher/Counselor participation: Leader.
    When we breathe, we typically only use the top half of our lungs. The most effective way to get oxygen into the body and relax it from negative emotional states is to stop, rearrange the body into an open and aligned position, and breathe slowly and deeply for a few minutes.
    Have students sit comfortably in their chair with their feet on the floor or lie on the ground in a position where nothing is obstructing their airway from the nose and mouth to the lungs. Sometimes closing their eyes helps students focus on their breath rather than on what they are upset about. This is helpful for students who are easily distracted. Talk students through breathing slowly in through their nose, filling up the bottom of their lungs first, and then breathing out through their mouth. When they are breathing correctly, their diaphragm, the muscle that lies at the bottom on the lungs, will move up and down. A good image for this is, "Pretend your lungs are balloons. You want to slowly blow up the balloon and when you do, your stomach will expand." [That's the diaphragm moving as the lungs are filling with air.] Start them off with a slow count of five for inhaling and exhaling, then slowly expand the count to 10 or 15.

The Four Part Breath

Goals addressed: Emotional Release, Stress Management, and Relaxation.
    Space requirements: Students can do this anywhere.
    Teacher/Counselor participation: Leader.

1. Breathe in through your nose to a slow count of four.
2. Hold your breath for four slow counts.

3. Breathe out through your mouth to a slow count of four.

4. Pause for four slow counts before you begin to breathe again.

Continue for several minutes until you feel calm.

Progressive Body Relaxation

Goals addressed: Emotional Release, Stress Management, and Relaxation.

Space requirements: Students can do this anywhere, but it works best if they are lying flat on the floor.

Teacher/Counselor participation: Leader.

Lying on their back with arms by their sides and legs flat on the floor, students start doing diaphragmatic breathing. With each inbreath, ask them to imagine they are breathing in relaxation and warmth. With each outbreath, ask them to imagine they are breathing out stress or allowing the stress to melt out of their bodies into the floor. Begin with the toes, and have them breathe all the way down into their toes to make them relaxed and warm. (Really, of course, they can't breathe farther down than their lungs, but the image of breathing into all parts of the body, really helps the muscles to relax.) Move from their toes to feet to lower legs to upper legs to lower back to abdomen to stomach to upper back to fingers to lower arms to upper arms to chest to shoulders to head. Periodically, remind them they are breathing in warmth and relaxation, and breathing out tension.

Progressive Body Relation Variations: Some people prefer to do a progressive relaxation from head to toes. Other people prefer to tense and release their muscles instead of using imagery. Discover what works best for your students.

Behavior Regulation

Behavior regulation involves the ability to make choices about what actions to take in response to one's own thoughts and emotions and the behavior of others. People who have poor behavior regulation react based on emotional responses. For example, a boy bumps into a girl in line. If the girl has poor behavior regulation, she might immediately turn around and push him back without investigating why he bumped into her. If she took the time to find out why he bumped into her, she may discover that he was pushed by another child, or he tripped and started to fall. The appropriate response to an accidental bump would be not to push back, but maybe to say, "That hurt" or "Are you OK?" If she discovered he had bumped into her deliberately, she might choose to push back or better yet, go tell an adult.

Body Boundaries

Sometimes conflicts occur in the classroom when students are unaware of personal boundaries. This can be true of students with sensorimotor difficulties who are not certain where their body begins and ends or of students who are preoccupied and not paying attention to where they are headed. Drama experiments that explore personal boundaries help students improve awareness of where they are in relation to others.

Hula Hoop Walk (Bubble Walk)

Goals addressed: Body Control, Personal Space, and Spatial Awareness.

Space requirements: An open space where students can move.

Teacher/Counselor participation: Coach.

Supplies required: One hula hoop for each participant. Hula hoops should be small enough that participants can stand in the middle and hold the hoop on two sides.

Explain that the hula hoops represent each person's personal space bubble. If our personal space bubbles are invaded by someone else without our permission, we often feel unsafe. Students move around the room, slowly at first, inside their hula hoop and practice avoiding others' hula hoops. If students are having difficulty moving smoothly, see if playing music with a flowing quality helps (perhaps "The Blue Danube Waltz" or "Clair De Lune"). Vary the speed at which students move once they become proficient at moving slowly.

If there are not enough hula hoops for everyone or there is not enough space for everyone to move with a hula hoop at the same time, split the class into smaller groups. Have one group practice while the other group watches.

Body Boundaries/Personal Space

Goals addressed: Body Awareness, Boundaries, Personal Space.

Space requirements: A place along the wall where students can stand in a line and be approached from about six feet away.

Teacher/Counselor participation: Coach and Boundary Measurer.

Supplies required: Something to mark personal space boundary, such as a pencil or piece of tape.

Students line up with their backs against the wall, standing two to three feet from each other. Explain:

> Personal space is a little bit different for everyone, but typically it is about the length of a person's arm in front of and all around them – almost like a personal bubble that we move in. If the boundary of personal space is broken without permission, a person can feel threatened. When we are sick or upset, we usually need more personal space. Since we want everyone to feel safe in this room, we are going to measure what everyone's personal space boundary is.

The Coach (and assistants if you have them) starts about six feet away from each student and slowly walks forward until both can sense the invisible boundary. Tell students to tell you to stop when they sense you have reached their personal space boundary. This gives them practice identifying it. You will be able to feel the boundary, too, in the body response of the student. It may be a tiny response, but it will be clear. Mark where that boundary is on the floor. After everyone's boundaries have been marked, compare them, and talk about the similarities and differences.

Helpful Hint: If you are much taller than the students, they may end up having larger than normal personal space measurements because there are larger personal space needs when a large person approaches a shorter one. If this is the case, you may want to use the idea in the helpful hint below so that the Measurer is closer to the same height as the Measured.

Helpful Hint: If there is only one Coach and many students, measuring the boundary of each can get boring for the waiting students. If you think your students can be serious about this experiment, you could enlist several of them to help you mark boundaries. Train them in sensing personal boundaries a day before doing the experiment.

Come-Go-Stay

Goals addressed: Body Awareness, Boundaries, Decision-making, Eye Contact, Following Directions, Non-Verbal Communication, Personal Space, and Teamwork.

Space requirements: A wall for students to line up against and an open space in front of it for students to move in.

Teacher/Counselor participation: Coach.

Number of players: Students work in pairs. Threesomes will not work for this experiment.

The group divides into pairs. One member of each pair lines up with back against the wall, shoulder to shoulder with others, facing into the room: They are the Senders. The other partners stand about six feet away, facing their Sender partner. They are the Receivers. The Senders put their hands behind their backs and use only their faces to send one of three messages to their Receiver: "Come," "Go," or "Stay (Stop)." No words or sounds are allowed. "Come" and "Go" messages indicate a direct line toward or away from the partner, not diagonally across the room (This is for safety, so Receivers do not bump into each other). The Senders remain at the wall; only the Receivers move. In addition, they should only move when they clearly understand the message being sent. Senders vary the messages they are sending. Whenever the Receiver reads a change in the communication, they respond to it.

After two or three minutes of sending and receiving, tell the Receivers to go back to where they started. Going down the line, pair by pair, ask each Receiver how many of the non-verbal messages they thought they understood. They can respond by percentage. For instance, "I think I got 80% of them," or "I think I got 4 out of 10." Then ask the Sender about how many messages the Receiver actually got correct. Sometimes the Sender will agree with the Receiver, but sometimes the Receiver has been correct more times than they thought. In this case, encourage the Receiver to trust their non-verbal observations. If they are correct less often than they thought, suggest that they need to practice their reading of nonverbal signals.

Once you have checked in with all pairs, the lines can reverse places and roles: The Senders become Receivers, and the Receivers become Senders. Play again for about two to three minutes, then check in with each pair. Follow this with a discussion about non-verbal communication.

Finding Spaces

Goals addressed: Attention, Body Control, Boundaries, Personal Space, and Spatial Awareness.

Space requirements: An open space where students can move.

Teacher/Counselor participation: Leader.

Players move around the room randomly and at different speeds determined by the Leader. Their purpose is to find the empty spaces in the room. This requires taking stock of where each player is and where they are moving, while also moving themselves. Obviously, this is an advanced exercise. Wait until you have observed strong personal boundary skills before allowing your students to play this game.

Inhibition or Impulse Control

Inhibition is the ability to stop or pause thought, emotion, or behavior by choice. Another name for inhibition is impulse control. This is a difficult skill for many young people. It can be particularly difficult for children who have ADHD, Obsessive Compulsive Disorder (OCD), or ASD. Being able to inhibit behavior is the beginning of behavior regulation. It provides a person with the time to think through the best way to respond. There may be many options of actions to take or just a few, but in any case, taking the time to make a thoughtful choice is also the beginning of mature behavior.

Freeze

Goals addressed: Body Control, Gross Motor Skills, Impulse Control (Inhibition), Listening Skills.

Space requirements: Open space in which students can move freely.

Teacher/Counselor participation: Leader.

Players walk around the room and stop completely whenever the Leader calls out, "Freeze!" They can move again when the leader says, "Unfreeze!" or "Go!"

Variation: Animal Transformations

If players need a lot of practice with freezing, there are many ways to vary this game to make it interesting. One way is to call out the name of different animals after each time they freeze. Then when they begin to move again, they must move and behave like the new animal.

Helpful Hint: For purposes of behavior management, it is very important to say, "If you are a ferocious or mean animal, you cannot attack another animal. You must stay in your own personal space."

Variation: Environment Walks

Call out different kinds of environments and weather that students have to walk through after each "Freeze." (For example: A jungle, a desert, the bottom of the sea, a driving rainstorm, etc.)

Variation: Shoe Walks

Call out shoes worn by different people after each "Freeze." Players then move as they would if they were wearing those shoes. (For example: cowboy boots, ballet slippers, high heels, tennis shoes, etc.)

Simon Says

Goals addressed: Body Control, Impulse Control (Inhibition), and Listening Skills.
   Space requirements: Open space.
   Teacher/Counselor participation: Leader.
   This is an old favorite that most people know how to play. It requires the players to do what Simon says *only* when the person being Simon says, "Simon says … " before issuing the command. If "Simon says … " is not included with the command, everyone should inhibit taking that action.

Jerusalem Jericho (Aycox, 1997)

Goals addressed: Attention, Impulse Control (Inhibition), and Listening Skills.
   Space requirements: Open space or students standing by their desks.
   Teacher/Counselor Participation: Leader.
   This is a variation of Simon Says, but sneakier because it depends on inhibiting one's movement until hearing the later syllables of the words. When the Leader bows and says "Jerusalem," the rest of the Players must bow at the same time. If the Leader bows and says, "Jericho," the players should not bow.
   Variation: To give different Players a turn being the Leader, each time someone bows when they are not supposed to or does not bow when they are supposed to, the Leader changes places with the person (or one of the people) who are not doing the appropriate action.

Sarvisilla (Nelson & Glass, 1992)

Goals addressed: Attention Impulse Control (Inhibition) and Listening Skills

Space requirements: Leader and players standing in a circle, by their desks, or in an open space.

Teacher/Counselor participation: Caller (Horner) and Coach.

This is a Finnish game, from the land of snow and reindeer, also in the tradition of Simon Says, but it requires players to listen carefully in a different way. The Leader (aka the Horner) stands facing the group, and says "Horns, horns, horns – [an animal with horns] buckhorns." At this players put their hands on either side of their heads and spread their fingers like deer horns. If the Horner says, "Horns, horns, horns – [an animal with no horns] doghorns," no one should make horns with their hands, just keep their hands at their sides.

If students have learned about all the different animals who have horns, the Horner could vary buckhorns with elkhorns, moosehorns, reindeerhorns, bisonhorns, ramhorns, or another animal that has horns. And for the no-horns category any animal that does not have horns could be used like elephanthorns, cathorns, mousehorns, etc.

If students make a mistake, encourage them to listen more carefully (as opposed to eliminating them). If they want to know how well they have listened, they could keep track of how many times they make a mistake and keep the score to compare with a playing of the game later on.

After players understand the game, the Horner role can be passed to a player.

Variation: The Horner could call out different animals and have students create the shape of the ears or horns of each one.

Head-Shoulders-Knees-Toes

Goals addressed: Body Control, Gross Motor Movement, Initiation, Inhibition, Opposite Action Skills, and Working Memory

Space requirements: Students could stand at their desks or in a circle.

Teacher/Counselor participation: Leader.

When the leader says, "Heads," students put their hands on their heads.

When the leader says, "Shoulders," students put their hands on their shoulders.

When the leader says, "Knees," students put their hands on their knees.

When the leader says, "Toes," students bend down and touch their toes.

Then the leader varies the order of the commands.

After a while, the leader reverses the commands.

When the leader says, "Heads," students bend down and touch their toes."

When the leader says, "Shoulders," students touch their knees.

When the leader says, "Knees," students touch their shoulders.

When the leader says, "Toes," students touch their heads.

Variation: Translate the body parts to be touched into French, Spanish, or another language.

Go Around Pantomimes

Goals addressed: Attention, Non-Verbal Communication, and Turn Taking.

Space requirements: Enough space for a circle of chairs.

Teacher/Counselor participation: Player.

A Go-Around game is just like it sounds: The group goes around the circle, and each one pantomimes an action related to a common category. Categories could include: Food, Snacks, Animals, Sports, Occupation, Summer Activity, Winter Activity, Fall Activity, Spring Activity, Weather, etc. If you have a category related to something you are studying in one of your academicsubjects, use that.

Start with one person, then go around the circle so everyone gets a turn. If someone cannot think of something to pantomime, they can pass and do their pantomime later. The group needs to watch each person's pantomime all the way through before they guess. If you have young students, you might want to allow them to make sounds as well.

You can have a rule that everyone must think of something different to pantomime, or if you have created a category like my pet or my favorite [something] there may be more than one person with the same creature or object to pantomime.

Civil Disobedience (Boal, 1992)

Goals addressed: Body Control, Impulse Control (Inhibition), Listening Skills, Opposite Actions.

Space requirements: Open space.

Teacher/Counselor participation: Leader.

This game was created by Brazilian theatre director Augusto Boal (1992). The Leader tells the group to do something, but they are supposed to do the opposite. Players are required to inhibit the commanded behavior, think of an opposite action, and initiate that action.

 ## Conclusion

The games offered in this chapter can be used to improve a variety of executive functions that students need for their academics. These games also assist in teaching students skills they can use as building blocks for social skills. Many of these games can serve as warm-ups to get students focused before jumping into games in later chapters and before academic tests. Education experts talk about the need for "Brain Breaks" during the school day so students can move their bodies, release excess energy, and even re-awaken parts of their brain that have temporarily "gone offline." Any of these games would be wonderful "Brain Breaks." They tend to be short, but get students up out of their chairs and engaging in learning through their whole bodies.

Notes

1. There are professional actors who use this outside-in approach to create emotions when they perform.

References

Aycox, F. (1997) *Games we should play in school, 2nd* ed. Front Row Experience.

Aspegren, E. (2020, August 8). "Feels like the world is against you": Young people struggle with finding mental health support amid COVID-19 pandemic. *USA Today*.

Bilodeau, L. (1992). *The anger workbook*, Hazelden Publishing.[AQ5]

Boal, A. (1992). *Games for actors and non-actors*. Routledge.

Bovard, K. (2000). The emotion map. *Teaching Tolerance*, 7(1), pp. 18–22. Available at: http://www.tolerance.org/magazine/number-17 -spring-2000/emotion-map

Chboskey, S. (Director). (2017). *Wonder [Film]*. Lionsgate, Mandeville Films.

Davis, A. (Director). (2003). *Holes. [Film]*. Walt Disney Films.

Delgado, R. (1986). *Acting with both sides of the brain*. Holt, Rinehard, & Winston.

Diamond, A., & Ling, D. S. (2016). Conclusions about interventions, programs, and approaches for improving executive functions that appear justified and those that, despite much hype, do not. *Developmental Cognitive Neuroscience 18*, pp. 34–48. Available at: http://dx.doi.org/10.1016/j.dcn.2015.11.005

Docter, P. (Director.) (2015). *Inside out. [Film]*. Pixar Animation Studios.

Evans, D. M. (Director). (1993). *The sandlot. [Film]*. Island World.

Goldberg, E. (2009). *The new executive brain: Frontal lobes in a complex world*. Oxford University Press.

Goleman, D. (2005) *Emotional intelligence: Why it can matter more than IQ*, (10th Anniversary Ed.). Bantam.

Holland, A. (1993). *The Secret Garden. [Film]*. American Zoetrope.

Howard, R. (Director). (1989) *Parenthood. [Film]*. Imagine Entertainment.

Klingberg, T. (2009). *The overflowing brain: Information overload and the limits of working memory*. Oxford University Press.

Marso, A. (2019, May 5). Mental health issues on rise for KC children. Kansas City Star, A1, A20.

Nelson, W. E., & Glass, H. (1992). *International playtime: Classroom games and dances from around the world*. Frank Schaffer Publications, Inc.

Russell, J. (Director). (2000). *My dog Skip. [Film]*. Alcon Entertainment.

Siegel, D. J. (1999). *The developing mind: How relationships and the brain interact to shape who we are*, Guilford Press.

Spolin, V. (1963). *Improvisation for the theatre*. Northwestern University Press.

Stanislavski, C. (1948). *An actor prepares*. Theatre Arts Books.

Stein, K. (2007). *The genius engine: Where memory, reason, passion, violence and creativity intersect in the human brain*. John Wiley & Sons, Inc.

Tavris, C. (1989) *Anger: The misunderstood emotion*, (rev. ed.). Simon & Schuster.

Vygotsky, L. S., (1978). *Mind in society: The development of higher psychological processes*. Harvard University Press.

Vygotsky, L. S. (1986). *Thought and language*. The MIT Press.

Building on Thinking and Social-Emotional Skills Through Drama

Once students learn how to handle the freedom inherent in drama activities, begin to cooperate and work together, and develop their executive functions, they can move on to drama games and improvisational activities that require more complex skills. As those skills improve, students will develop the ability to focus and sustain attention for longer periods of time. Their impulse control, patience, and turn-taking abilities will improve, as will their abilities to sequence and listen effectively. With a little re-directing, these new strengths can be applied to academic areas, such as taking in and following academic instructions, using language more articulately to express ideas, and understanding the relationships between concepts.

The first two sections of this chapter contain drama explorations that build on some of the executive functions worked on in the last chapter. These games need a higher level of skill and more frustration tolerance than the ones in Chapter Two, which is why they are listed here. The next three sections provide explorations to assist students in developing communication skills, the ability to think critically, make good choices, and work successfully in groups. Some beginning improvisation is involved in these explorations. Students should be able to transition into these activities without specific improvisation instruction, but if you find your students struggling with an activity, refer to Chapter Four, which addresses the basic rules of improvisation.

Improved Turn Taking, Impulse Control, and Sequencing

Improved ability to take turns when playing a game or having a conversation requires impulse control. A number of games were shared in the last chapter for improving impulse control. As a result, turn-taking abilities should have grown.

Often, the younger children are, the more difficult it can be to wait their turn and focus on others; nevertheless, learning to be less self-focused is part of growing up. Drama games can be a pleasurable way to learn how to share experiences and move from associative to cooperative play, since expressive activities are entertaining to watch as well as do.

Waiting for a turn can become easier when, while waiting, participants are engaged and encouraged to learn from the work others are doing. Try reframing the time between turns as the part of the game when students can enjoy each other's acting and learn from each other, instead of it being time they are "just waiting." Give the turn waiters something to identify or evaluate while others are taking their turns. Depending on the game and focus abilities of the students, check in with the group after every person's turn finishes or after the round is completed to see what they observed.

When working on the enhancement of turn taking, be aware that some students are not good at waiting for their turn because they have a deficit of attention. By this I do not mean they have a neurological disorder like attention deficit hyperactivity disorder (ADHD); I mean that they have not had enough attention given to them by significant adults at home. As a result, they are craving to be in the spotlight. These are often the students who become the class clowns. Their deficit of attention might be happening for a number of reasons. The student's family might be under great stress, and parents (or a single parent) are holding down several jobs to keep a roof over their heads. There could be a family member who has become the focus of all the attention to the detriment of the others. That person could be very ill, in trouble with the law, or have a serious disability. Resources and attention are being targeted to this person for good reason, and others in the household feel left out. They are not supposed to feel jealous or angry, but they do. Their social and affiliative needs are not being met at home. This kind of deficit of attention can make it difficult for these children to wait for their time in the spotlight. You may find that doing at least one drama activity a day helps these students get their attention needs addressed. You might also find other ways to involve these students during the week so their deficits of attention begin to be met, and they feel as if they are valuable, contributing members of the classroom.

Count 1–20

Goals addressed: Attention, Impulse Control, Initiation, Listening, Nonverbal Communication, Sequencing, and Turn Taking.

Space requirements: Students could be at their desks, but the game will be more effective if they are in a circle facing each other.

Teacher/Counselor participation: Player and Coach.

The group stands in a circle and counts from 1 to 20 (or to a lower number if the group is younger) without a pre-arranged order of speaking. If two people speak at the same time, the group must start over at one. Not only must the players know which number comes next in the sequence, they must listen to each other to sense when to speak.

This game and the next are in this chapter because when students first begin to work together, they are not yet tuned into each other. Therefore, sensing when to speak can be difficult. Some groups can become very frustrated if they end up going back to one repeatedly without getting to the end number.

Helpful Hint: If you have students who jump in constantly and do not give others a chance to say a number, you can make a rule that everyone in the group has to say a number before anyone can say a second one. This will also encourage shy students who have been holding back to participate.

Variation: ABC through Z

The group stands in a circle and tries to say the alphabet from A to Z in no pre-arranged speaking order. If two people speak at the same time, the group must start over at A. The group must listen to each other to sense when to speak.

Helpful Hint: Since the alphabet has 26 letters, you might want to start with students working to get from A to L and then M to Z, so they can achieve some success early on. Then try going from beginning to end.

Please note: It is cheating if students follow a set pattern, like going around the circle or jumping in a prearranged order. The point of this game is the connection that is made among the group listening to each other and working together to achieve their goal.

Go

Goals addressed: Attention, Attention Shifting, Boundaries, Eye Contract, Following Directions, Initiation, Impulse Control (Inhibition), Opposite Action, and Working Memory.

Space requirements: Enough space for the group to stand in a circle.

Teacher/Counselor participation: Participant or coach.

Player One makes eye contact with a second Player in the circle. Player Two gives Player One permission to move to his/her spot by saying, "Go." Player One starts walking toward Player Two's place. Now Player Two must move to a new place in the circle. Player Two looks at a third person in the circle. Player Three gives Player Two permission to move by saying, "Go." As Player Two is moving toward Player Three, Player Three must now get permission to move to a new space. And so on.

The difficulty in this game is that the player who has just given permission cannot move until *they* have permission to move. Having just said the word, "Go," one's tendency is to begin to move. But no movement can happen until the *next* person says, "Go."

Helpful Hint: Have players move *very slowly* (maybe even in slow motion) the first time you play this to give the player who has just said go, enough time to shift attention from giving permission to getting permission from another.

This game is a very advanced game and will only be successful if all players are alert and on their toes!

Inappropriate or Appropriate?

Goals addressed: Decision-making, Improvisation Skills, Impulse Control, Opposite Action Skills, Social Skills, and Verbal Expression.

Space requirements: This could be done at students' desks or in a circle of chairs.

Teacher/Counselor participation: Leader and Coach.

Supplies required: Different situations in which a person might say something rude or inappropriate written on a slip of paper, Simple props for the scenes.

Students each pick a slip of paper. They have to identify something inappropriate that someone might think and say in this situation, and then they have to identify what would be appropriate to say instead. If a student cannot think of something appropriate to say or do in this situation, the class can help with ideas. A short scene can be acted out to practice responding in the appropriate manner.

Improved Attention, Working Memory, and Body Awareness

For improvisation to be successful, students need to be able to pay attention, remember what has recently been said or done to keep the scene on track, and control their bodies so that they do not bump into other actors unintentionally. Many attention skills are built from drama games that also improve working memory. These often enhance listening skills as well (although there will be a section specifically on improving listening skills later in this chapter). This section contains games that are a little more advanced than the metacognitive games in Chapter Two.

Telephone

Goals addressed: Attention, Listening Skills, and Working Memory.

Space requirements: Enough space for group to sit in a circle in chairs.

Teacher/Counselor participation: Coach.

Supplies suggested: If you want to reinforce a lesson from one of your academic lessons, you could have phrases relating to that lesson typed up on slips of paper for students to pick from.

The group sits in a circle. Player One makes up a phrase (or chooses a phrase from a slip of paper) and whispers it to a player on their right or left. The phrase is passed around the circle, and when it gets to the last player, that person says what they heard out loud. If the group has been paying attention, listening carefully, and using their working memories, the phrase will be the same.

If the phrase is different, discover where it changed and if it changed more than once. A word of caution needs to be injected here; however, because students are often so afraid of being wrong or making a mistake, they may say the "correct answer" after they hear it, instead of what they actually said. I am not suggesting that students are dishonest, but some may worry that they will be blamed for "ruining" the game by the other students if they were the only one who "messed up." In addition, students who do have working memory issues may actually forget what they really said once they hear the original phrase. To avoid putting anyone on the spot, start with the last player and go backwards around the circle, having each player say what they remember hearing and passing on. Approach this discovery process as if you are a group of scientists solving a mystery, instead of a police force searching for a criminal.

Articulation Practice

Consonants create the "shape" or the "skeleton" of words. Said in another way, consonants, "make the spoken word intelligible," especially those that are at the end of syllables (Lessac, 1967, p. 129). Arthur Lessac, who developed the Lessac System of voice and diction, said:

> When consonants are changed or lost, the whole word is changed or lost. Without a properly executed T, the word *wrote* may very well be heard as *rode, rogue, roan, roam, rope, robe, role, rove, rose, roast,* or *roach* … Your speech will improve almost at once if you remember and abide by the rule that while there is some tolerance for error in producing vowels, there is practically no tolerance for error in producing consonants.
>
> (Lessac, 1967, p. 129)

There are a number of consonants, called cognates, which are made in identical ways with the lips, tongue and/or mouth. For instance, b and p are both made with the lips in a similar configuration, but b is voiced using the vocal chords and p is created with the breath and not the vocal chords. This is true also for:

d and t

g and k

v and f

z and s

and there are four sets of dipthongs:

th as in brea*the* versus th as in brea*th*

zh as in plea*s*ure versus sh as in wi*sh*

dg as in ju*dg*e versus ch as in *church*

dz as in inten*ds* versus ts as in physici*sts*

Words using these consonant sounds can be misheard if the speaker does not take enough time to complete and/or voice the sounds of the first of the cognate pair (b, d, g, v, z, th, zh, dg, dz) or if they *do* voice the sound of the second of the cognate pair (p, t, k, f, s, th, sh, ch, ts) (Lessac, 1967, p. 134).

The Leader can create phrases that involve words using these consonants and cognates. This will challenge students to use their articulation skills as well as their listening skills when they play Telephone.

Backwriting (A Tactile Version Of Telephone)

Goals addressed: Attention Skills, Sensory Integration, Sequencing, Teamwork, and Turn taking.

Space requirements: A large enough space to make four to six parallel lines of students.

Teacher/Counselor participation: Leader.

Create four to six straight lines of players. The lines should be parallel with each other, and the players in each line should be facing forward. The Leader thinks of a list of four, five, or six letter words (depending on the number of lines). The Leader traces one letter of the word on the back of each player at the end of the line with the index finger. If the player does not recognize the letter, they can ask for it to be re-traced.

Helpful hint: Since in English reading moves from left to right, be sure to trace the letters in the opposite order at the end of the line (right to left) so that they end up in the correct order when they reach the front of the line.

After all the last players in line have their letter, the Leader says, "Go," and they start passing their letter down the line. Players can ask to have the letter re-traced if they do not think they understand it. Then they pass it to the person in front of them. Accuracy is more important than speed in this game.

When the letter gets to the front of each line, the first person in line should either write it down on a small piece of paper or quietly whisper it to the Leader who has moved to the front of the line. When all letters have arrived at the front, each player from left to right will say out loud what letter they thought they got. If all the letters were recognized and passed correctly, they will spell the word.

This game could be played competitively by giving points to lines each time they get their letter in the word correct, but it is often more fun for everyone if it is just about trying to work together to spell out the word.

This could be a great exercise to do when introducing new spelling words or when practicing for a spelling or vocabulary quiz.

The Captain is Coming

Goals addressed: Body Control, Following Directions, Listening Skills, Spatial Awareness, Teamwork, and Working Memory.

Space requirements: A large, open space in which students can move.

Teacher/Counselor participation: Caller (Captain) and Coach.

The Caller begins as the Captain and calls out a variety of commands. Players/Sailors have actions to take for each command or formation:

"The Captain is Coming!" Everyone stands at attention and salutes the Captain.

"To the Ship!" Everyone moves to the right side of the room.

"To the Shore!" Everyone moves to the left side of the room.

"Man Overboard!" Two Sailors: One drops to one knee and the other stands behind with one hand on the kneeling one's shoulder. Both scan the sea for the man overboard with their hands shading their eyes.

"Crow's Nest!" Three Sailors stand back to back and lock arms at the elbow to form the crow's nest.

"Mess Table!" Four Sailors sit at each side of an imaginary square table and pretend to eat ravenously, making loud obnoxious eating sounds.

"Walk the Plank!" Five Sailors stand in a line single file with their hands on the shoulders of the Sailor in front of them (except, of course, for the first Sailor).

To avoid Sailors pushing, shoving, and running to get into a formation, ask them to focus on remembering the number of Sailors required for each formation. Accuracy is more important than speed for the purposes of improving working memory (and safer). If there are extra Sailors left over after a formation is made, that's OK. They are not "out." Have them help you carefully check all the groups to see if any of the configurations need another Sailor. If one is needed, they can join it, and if not, they can join back in the game the next round.

If players have working memory or auditory processing difficulties, start playing the game with the first three or four commands. Add others later. This is the type of game that students love so much, they want to play it again and again, so there will be time to learn all the formations.

Other formations can be created to add to these OR an entirely different version can be invented. For instance, for a class studying about Robin Hood, commands could be "Robin's Coming!" "To Sherwood!" "To Nottingham," and different formations could be created for important moments or places in the story. For a class studying nutrition, commands could be "The Head Chef's coming!" "To the Kitchen!" "To the Dining Room!" and different formations could be invented for each food group. While working on a play about Candyland, the choreographer created a version of this game where each formation was a different kind of cake or candy. "Twizzlers" was each person individually standing tall and twisting their legs and arms up!

Finding Your Partner With A Sound

Goals addressed: Body Control, Listening Skills, Sensory Awareness, and Spatial Awareness.

Space requirements: Large open space where students can move.

Teacher/Counselor participation: Coach and Spotter.

Supplies required: Blindfolds for each player.

The class divides into pairs. Each pair decides on a sound they will make to find each other (same sound so they match). Listen to all the sounds and make sure they are different. Have partners split up and go to opposite sides of the room. If you can trust your students to keep their eyes closed, great. If not, use blindfolds. Students begin making their sounds, quietly enough that the different sounds can be heard. They move toward each other slowly, trying to get nearer to the sound, but also trying not to bump into other people. Because others are making a noise as they move, it is possible to avoid them. When all the pairs find each other, the round is over.

Helpful Hint: If you want some students to serve as spotters to keep blindfolded students safe, have half of the class play at a time.

Helpful Hint: Make sure that this game is not done as a competition with the winners being the first pairs to find each other. That will cause students to run or rush toward their partner's sound, and they will end up either bumping into others or tripping, falling, and hurting themselves.

Santa's Elves

Goals addressed: Listening Skills and Sensory Awareness.

Space requirements: Players standing in a large circle.

Teacher/Counselor participation: Player.

Supplies needed: Blindfolds.

Everyone stands in a circle, facing in. One person volunteers to be It and stands in the center of the circle blindfolded. The Players walk around the circle singing a song. It could be Jingle Bells or another song everyone knows from any time of the year. At the end of the song, the group stops. The Player immediately in front of It asks, "What would you like for Christmas?" or "Have you been good this year?" or another question that one of Santa's Elves might ask. However, they disguise their voice so that they do not sound as they normally do. It has to guess who is speaking. If It can guess who it is, that Player and It change places. If It guesses incorrectly, he or she must remain in the center.

Helpful Hint: If you have a class that is stellar at making up funny voices, you could give It three guesses. After all, the Miller's Daughter had three opportunities to guess Rumplestiltskin's name.

Helpful Hint: If the player who is It does not guess after three rounds of the game, asks for a volunteer to take their place.

Helpful Hint: If you would rather not use Santa's Elves for the Players in the circle, or if you feel that this limits what time of the year you could play this game, you could re-name the game The Royal Servants or Robin Hood's Merry Men and Women. Funny voices could still be used, and Players would ask the kind of questions that those characters might ask.

Problem-solving

Magic Stick/Magic Tube

Goals addressed: Attention, Decision-making, Generating Alternatives, Cognitive Flexibility, Non-verbal Communication, Observation Skills, Problem-solving, Turn-taking, and Working Memory.

Space requirements: This experiment works best when players are standing in a large circle. If your students will get restless standing, let them sit in chairs, but make sure they know they can get up during their turn.

Teacher/Counselor participation: Player and Coach.

Supplies needed: A stick, paper towel tube, pencil, frisbee, cup, basket, or other object.

The group stands in a circle. Each player takes a turn acting out what the object could be, based on its shape and the way it is being used in pantomime. The group guesses what that object is, then the object is passed onto the next person. For instance, a paper towel tube could become a stick of dynamite, a violin bow, an arrow, or a really large tooth-brush, depending on how it is used by the player. Students can play this game for hours!

This game is useful when a group is having difficulty solving a problem together because they cannot agree on one answer, they cannot think of any answer, or they are not willing to take each other's perspectives.

Helpful Hint: A paper towel tube is better to use than a stick because it is not harmful it if hits someone or if it is thrown (as a javelin or lance). If it is broken, it's not a great loss because it's just a cardboard tube. It can be decorated to look "magical" with acrylic paint or colored tape. I recommend avoiding glitter, wonderful as it is, because it always flakes off. Typically, I have at least two magic paper towel tubes with me when playing the game, in case one gets destroyed.

Variation: Magic Scarf

Supplies needed: Large piece of fabric.

What makes this game a little different from the previous one is that a large piece of fabric is malleable and can be formed into different shapes. The Magic Scarf can become any number of pieces of clothing, but it can also become a bed, a baby, a blanket, a fire, a door: A much greater variety of objects than something that cannot change its shape.

Partner Pantomimes

Goals addressed: Attention, Cognitive Flexibility, Decision-making, Generating Alternatives, Initiation, Non-verbal Communication, Observation Skills, Problem-solving, Social Connection, Turn-taking, Teamwork, and Working Memory.

Space requirements: Large circle with chairs.

Teacher/Counselor participation: Coach and Player.

Students think of an activity (within good taste) that one person cannot do alone, but needs one or more other people to help them do. When they have an idea, they come to the middle of the circle and begin doing one person's part of the action in pantomime (no words or sounds). As soon as someone figures out how they need help, they can get up and help. For instance, two people could create a teeter totter, three people could create a jump rope, four people could create a card game, and a large group of people could create a baseball team.

A good discussion to have after playing this game is to talk about the importance of asking for help if you need it. Other people cannot read your mind or might be focused on something else and not see that you need help. There is no shame in asking for help when you need it.

Scene With Three Props

Goals addressed: Attention, Decision-making, Generating Alternatives, Cognitive Flexibility, Non-verbal Communication, Problem-solving, Task Planning, Organization, etc., Teamwork, Verbal Communication, and Working Memory.

Space requirements: Enough space that small groups can sit together and plan.

Teacher/Counselor participation: Coach.

Supplies required: Many different objects from around your classroom, house, etc.

Divide your class into small groups of three or four. Each group will work together to create an original story using three props to inspire and be used in the story.

There are two different ways of dealing out the objects. The Coach can put three disparate objects in a paper bag and let each group pick a different bag, OR the Coach can lay out all the different objects on a table and let each group pick three. When I let the group pick objects themselves, I give them a choice to have one person be their object picker or have three people each pick an object. To avoid a rush at the objects and behavior akin to a Black Friday sale, have the object picker(s) choose one object at a time, take it back to their group, and return to the table. Do not let it become a free for all.

The groups have a given amount of time to come up with a story that involves all of the objects. Depending on the time available for the activity, either the group can tell their story, or they can act their story out. Scenes can be in pantomime with no words or with spoken dialogue, depending on the experience and comfort of the group.

Helpful Hint: If you have played Magic Tube/Magic Stick or Magic Scarf, you can tell students that they do not have to use the objects as what they are, but can use them as something their shape suggests. I had one incredible creative drama group who used a large rawhide bone as a dog bone, a broken leg, and a crutch all in the same scene.

Helpful Hint: If students ask how long their story or scene should be, tell them that each story will be different. There is no correct length – it should be as long as it needs to be to tell the story.

Communication Skills: Listening and Responding

Listening skills combine auditory processing, sensory integration, attenuation, sequencing, and other executive functioning processes. These are crucial for understanding instructions in class, at home, and in future jobs. Misunderstandings based on mishearing information will impact learning and social relationships negatively.

Each of us has a basic human need to feel validated and witnessed when we share something in a conversation. When this happens, we feel valued and taken seriously. However, those feelings will not happen if the listener:

1. does not acknowledge what we just said, and instead starts talking about something else,

2. does not know how to listen empathetically, or

3. responds with an inappropriate emotional reaction (like laughing at a sad tale or crying at a happy one).

Disconnects like these happen when a listener has not really paid attention to the words, facial expressions, and body messages of the speaker. Someone with ADHD might be distracted by something else going on in the room. The listener might be "in their own head" worrying about something that has nothing to do with what is being talked about. Someone who is concerned about impressing others might be thinking about what they will say next. Unfortunately, this is can even be a problem with adults who never learned that conversation is a give and take, back and forth effort. To listen well, the listener needs to ground themself in the present moment, and then focus on the speaker, working to hear what is being said.

On the other side of the coin, speakers will have a better chance of being understood if they know how to express what they feel, explain what happened to them, or ask for what they need clearly and articulately. Sequencing a story from beginning to end is important. If they jump around in their story, the listeners will get confused. If they lose the thread of their story and go down "rabbit trails," the listeners will get bored and miss the point of the story. Learning story structure will help with both of those problems, but in addition to learning about story structure, communicators need to practice, practice, and practice.

The following structured interactions provide students with practice in the back and forth of communicating a message, listening, and responding appropriately.

Listening With Drums/Percussion (Rhythmic Conversations)

Goals addressed: Attention, Listening Skills, Non-verbal Communication, and Rhythm.

Space requirements: This experiment can be done with students in pairs sitting face to face.

Teacher Counselor participation: Coach.

Supplies required: A drum or rhythm instrument for each student.

Student pairs sit facing each other. One begins a short rhythm, then stops. The second tries to copy the rhythm as closely as possible. Then the second takes a turn to make a different rhythm, and the first tries to copy it as closely as possible. They can continue for a set amount of time. When pairs are done, discuss if they felt their partner was really listening to the rhythm they made.

Variation: Drumming/Percussion Conversation

Student pairs sit facing each other. One begins a short rhythm. The second responds to the rhythm with a new rhythm of their own (or with a change in volume or pace). Students go back and forth, developing a rhythmic "conversation." When they are done, discuss if they felt as if they were communicating back and forth. If not, why was it not a successful communication? It may be at first that some pairs are trying to out-drum each other, which would not be an example of a constructive conversation with give and take. Instead, it is an example of bullying or fighting.

Variation: Drumming/Percussion Conversation on a Topic

Try a drumming or percussion conversation based on a topic. When the conversation is done, ask what they feel they "said" to each other and what they think "happened" by the end of the conversation. See if both partners had the same idea about their conversation. If they did not, this could lead to a good discussion about how we can misinterpret what others are saying.

Conversation Practice

Goals addressed: Attention, Flexibility, and Listening Skills.

Space requirements: This experiment can be done with students in pairs sitting face to face.

Teacher/Counselor participation: Coach.

Supplies suggested: If you think your students will not be able to decide on a topic to discuss, provide them with a sheet of prompts of appropriate conversation topics.

Students sit facing each other and decide on a topic of conversation. It could be about something that is currently happening, a made up situation, or you could have them pretend to be two characters in a story you are studying who are discussing an aspect of the story. One student starts the conversation, and the other listens. When the second student speaks, their response should relate to what the first student said. When the first speaker responds to the second, they should build on what the second person said.

Learning to listen carefully can be difficult. One way to introduce this exercise is to ask two students, who you think have good listening skills, to demonstrate how to build a conversation. Talk with the class about what happened during the conversation. Were they talking about the same thing? If one asked the other a question, was the question answered or ignored?

Another option is to have two students read an example of a conversation with careful listening and constructive responding:

ONE: I think I'm going to starve to death if we don't go to lunch soon.
TWO: I'm really hungry, too.
ONE: I hope we have pizza for lunch.
TWO: Me, too.
ONE: Is pizza your favorite lunch?
TWO: Just about. I like peanut butter and jelly sandwiches, too. But today I feel like pizza.
ONE: My favorite topping is sausage. What's yours?
TWO: Bacon!

Contrast it with a similar conversation where the speakers are not listening to each other:

ONE: I think I'm going to starve to death if we don't go to lunch soon.
TWO: I hate math. I think I'm going to flunk this year.
ONE: I love it when we can get seconds.
TWO: My dog ran away last night, and then we got him back.
ONE: I got a B on my spelling test yesterday.
TWO: I ate one of his dog biscuits once. It wasn't too bad.
ONE: I hope I don't get in trouble. Oh, I'm so hungry my stomach hurts.
TWO: I can't wait to get home to see my mom.

The second exchange is not really a conversation; it is more like two monologues going on at the same time. The two speakers do not respond to what the other says. They are speaking past each other, not with each other.

The conversation students practice does not need to be long. Especially the first few times this experiment is done. If several pairs of students are conversing at the same time, each pair could record their conversation on an iPad or phone and play it back for the class.

Ask students about their conversation. Did they feel the other person was listening and responding to what they were saying? If not, why? Listen to the recording. They may hear things in the recording that they did not realize they said or did, both positively and negatively. It is always preferable for a person to identify what went wrong themselves. Self-discoveries motivate us to improve more than criticism or analysis from others. After each student in the pair responds, ask the other students in class if they heard anything else.

Giving/Taking Directions To Build A Design

Goals addressed: Attention, Listening Skills, Sequencing, Task Planning, and Organization.

Space requirements: Partners working together at desks.

Teacher/Counselor participation: Coach.

Supplies needed: Either Legos of different colors and sizes or colored paper shapes and sheets of paper. A shield or blind to block one of the partners from seeing what the other partner is describing. This could be created out of corrugated cardboard that is folded so that it stands up. If using Legos, each pair of students should get two sets of the same blocks. If using colored shapes on colored paper, one student of each pair should have the shapes glued onto a piece of paper (perhaps placed in a large manila envelope so the partner cannot see it) and the other should have the shapes loose, a sheet of paper, and glue.

If using Legos: One student builds a shape with their blocks behind the blind. Then that student describes verbally for their partner how to build the same shape out of their set of Legos. The Describer should not watch the Builder so there is no temptation to correct how directions are being followed.

If using shapes of paper, the partner who received the glued down design describes to the partner how to arrange the shapes in the same manner on their piece of paper.

When the partners have finished arranging their Legos or paper shapes, remove the blind in between them to see how closely the designs match.

Helpful Hint: To teach this experiment to the class, the Coach may want to be the first describer (Practice first on friends or family at home!)

to everyone in the class. This will insure that the class understands exactly what is expected. If you make a mistake in your description, please, be willing to own it!

Helpful Hint: Start with very simple designs made with few pieces and work toward more complex designs with more pieces. The more your students are directionally challenged (right/left, up/down, vertical/horizontal), the easier you will want the early designs to be, so students can achieve success in the beginning.

Helpful Hint: Instead of focusing on right and wrong or assigning blame to who did not communicate clearly or listen carefully, discuss how communication and miscommunication happened from a perspective of curiosity. Focus on how difficult good communication really is and why it is so important to describe what you want or what you mean clearly. Remind students that if what someone says is confusing, it is ok to ask for clarification.

Group Storytelling

Goal addressed: Attention, Cognitive Flexibility, Decision-making, Generating Alternatives, Listening Skills, Sequencing, Verbal Communication, Turn-taking, and Working Memory.

Space requirements: Enough space for the group to sit or stand in a circle.

Teacher/Counselor participation: Player and Coach.

The group stands or sits in a circle. One Teller starts a story, and after setting the scene and the characters, the first Teller stops. The next Teller in the circle continues the story for a while, then passes it on to the next one, and so on, until the story ends. Everyone must remember what was said from the beginning of the story, so it continues to make sense. This is a less structured, more advanced version of Fortunately-Unfortunately that was presented in Chapter Two. If your students have not played Fortunately-Unfortunately, start with that game first.

Advanced Variation: One-Word Stories

The group stands or sits in a circle. One-word stories are built by the group one word at a time. This requires careful listening to make complete sentences that are not endless and make sense.

Advanced Variation: Two-Word Stories and Other Patterns

The group stands or sits in a circle. Build a story with each player being able to say two or three words before passing it on to the next player. This can be easier than one-word stories, but it can be difficult to keep track of how many words the speaker contributes or to limit the number of words to just two or three.

Another way to play this is to start with one word, then allow each person to use two words, then three words, and so on.

Tone of Voice Practice

Goals addressed: Listening Skills, Non-verbal Communication, and Verbal Communication

Space requirements: Students could work in pairs at desks or stand in pairs to give them more room for expressive movement.

Teacher/Counselor participation: Coach.

Create a two-line dialogue for students that they repeat again and again, changing the tone of voice to change the meaning. They can change the pace, the volume, the emotion, and the rhythm of the words to change the meaning. Adding their bodies in often helps tone of voice expression.

It is helpful to come up with a situation and relationship for the dialogue. Some of the examples below are obviously child and parent, but other relationships can be created as well.

Examples:

Each student picks a different color that they want to paint the walls of the room. The only word they need to say is the color. They try to convince the other to agree to that color. Finally, one can agree to end the dialogue

A: Blue
B: Green

A: I want to go to the store.
B: Later.

A: Can we have a puppy?
B: Ask your dad.

A: Give it to me!
B: I want it!

A: Mine!

B: No, mine!

A: Go to bed.

B: Not yet.

A: Yes.

B: No.

You can also have each student have a conversation using only their partner's name and have the class guess what their relationship is and what is happening between them.

The Snail (Cattanach, 1992)

Goals addressed: Cognitive Flexibility, Decision-making, Generating Alternatives, Improvisation Skills, Listening Skills, Problem-solving, Social Skills, and Verbal Communication.

Space requirements: Small open area.

Teacher/Counselor participation: Coach.

Supplies required: Large piece of fabric.

One student volunteers to be the Snail and hides in the shell (under the large piece of fabric). The student playing the Snail needs to agree to come out of the shell if a reason offered makes sense. The Snail does not succeed if it stays stubbornly in its shell – communication is the point of the game.

Another student volunteers to convince the Snail to come out of its shell. Both students need to listen carefully to each other and respond to what the other says. They should also pay attention to the emotional messages being sent by the tone of voice of the other speaker. That is part of the communication. If the Convincer can figure out what the Snail needs and meet those needs, there will be more chance of success.

There are several ways to handle this game, depending on your students:

- A time limit can be given for the Convincer to succeed with the Snail. When the Convincer succeeds or time is up, two new volunteers can take up the challenge.

- The Convincer role could rotate to a different student after each try or after a certain amount of time, with the Snail remaining in the game until a Convincer develops a strong rapport, and the Snail hears a reason it accepts as a good one for coming out.

- In popcorn fashion, students in the class could come forward to try to convince the Snail to come out of its shell. In this way, a number of different approaches can be tried, and everyone is kept active in the process.

Discussion can be held after the Snail comes out or after each convincing attempt, depending on the needs and abilities of the group.

Learning to Make Choices and Think Critically

Every school year, students have a great deal of information to learn in many different academic disciplines, leaving them little time for learning how to evaluate that information. Professors in universities lament the lack of critical thinking skills in first-year college students. I have sat in many faculty workshops listening to instructors bemoan the fact that college students do not know how to think for themselves, make choices, or take responsibility for their learning. I believe this may stem from students not having enough opportunities to practice evaluation and critical thinking skills pre-college. Often this is not the fault of their teachers, who have been put under unrelenting pressure by state and federal legislation, to teach to the standardized test.

There are a few simple drama experiments that can begin to teach even young students how to make choices and develop pride in thinking on their own. These experiments can be used for Brain Breaks during the school day, or they can be tied to academics. In any case, allowing students to make choices about what they think about the material they are learning can encourage them to become actively involved in discussions and more engaged in learning.

Decisions, Decisions! (Dano Beal, 2014)

Goals addressed: Critical Thinking, Decision-making, and Self-Awareness.

Space requirements: An open space in the room, perhaps divided down the middle with a line of masking tape on the floor or divided by some other identifier.

Teacher/Counselor participation: Caller and Coach.

Supplies suggested: Masking tape.

Students stand in the middle of the room. The Caller provides two choices within a category, and players get to pick between the two choices. Each round, the Caller designates the right side of the room for one choice and the left side for the other. Students move to the side of the room that matches their choice. Categories can be likes or dislikes: school subjects (Math or English?), colors (Orange or Blue?), animals (Rhinoceros or Hippopotamus?), pastimes (Basketball or Hide and Seek?). In addition to energizing students and allowing them to practice making choices, they will get to know each other better, and you will get to know them better.

To connect this game to academics, options of the answers chosen could be offered as a pre-test of material you are going to cover that day to see what they already know about the subject, or you could ask about material you have recently taught to see how much they remember. This also could be a way to review for a test in a way that physically engages students and wakes them up. In the same vein, after learning about a new subject area, students could be given choices about what would they like to learn more about.

After each choice is made, the Caller could move on to the next set of choices or ask students on each side why they chose that side. This gives them experience with supporting their choices.

Four Corners

Goals addressed: Critical Thinking, Decision-making, and Self-Awareness.

Space requirements: An open space in the room, perhaps divided in quarters with two lines of masking tape on the floor or some other physical identifier.

Teacher/Counselor participation: Caller and Coach.

Each corner of the space represents a different choice. The Leader provides four choices to the players. Which is your favorite season: Fall, Winter, Spring, or Summer? What is your favorite pet: Dog, Cat, Fish, or Bird? Have students support their choices.

Locograms (Also Called Categorical Groupings)

Goals addressed: Critical Thinking, Decision-making, Self-Awareness, and Social Connection.

Space requirements: Large open space.

Teacher/Counselor participation: Caller and Coach.

A locogram is a sociometric measurement done by players grouping into categories. Loco = location and gram = measurement.

The leader calls out different categories that players may be, like, prefer, agree with, disagree with, or hate, and the players must get into groups with others who have the same choice as they do. For instance, if the category is favorite desserts, players might yell out "ice cream," "cake," "pie," "brownies," etc. and form groups around these categories. Players find others who have commonalities with them.

Usually, the leader calls out the main category and allows the players to talk to each other and find who are in the same category as they are. Each group should clearly be in a separate space from others.

Sometimes it is hard to find a group to be part of if you like or hate more than one of the choices. For instance, someone might like chocolate and rocky road ice cream, but the other players have created separate groups, even though both kinds of ice cream have chocolate in them. That means the player with two favorites needs to make a choice between which they like more.

If several players like (or dislike) categories that are related to each other in some way, they could negotiate with their groups to re-locate close to each other. The players who like both could make their own group in between. This allows students to start thinking about relationships between categories.

If only one person likes a certain category, that is OK. There can be a group of one.

Variation: Categories In Order

Goals addressed: Decision-making, Self-Awareness, and Sequencing.

Space requirements: Have room for students to move to different spaces in the room to indicate their choices. Amount of space will depend on number of categories being asked about.

Teacher/Counselor participation: Caller and Coach.

Supplies required: It is helpful to have a sign naming the category in each part of the room so it is easily found.

The Caller decides on categories: subjects in school, personal strengths, personal weaknesses, athletic skills, etc. and each round students sort themselves into the appropriate category. In round one, students go to their strongest category, in round two they go to their next strongest, etc. This is a way for students to evaluate themselves in a variety of levels. This is interesting on several fronts. The teacher or counselor gets a stronger sense of what the students think about their skills. The students see who believe they have similar strengths or preferences as they do.

Helpful hint: Everyone does not always evaluate themselves accurately. Some people think their abilities are stronger than they actually are. This is called the *Dunning-Kruger effect* (Kruger & Dunning, 1999). Some people overestimate their knowledge and believe they are experts. This can lead some students to not bother studying for tests. Then they are surprised when they get a poor grade. Because they believe they are already superior, they are unable to recognize their mistakes and realize they need to work harder. This does not mean they are stupid; they have a blind spot or cognitive bias that makes them feel overconfident about skills they really need to work at.

Other people think their abilities are worse than they actually are. This is called the *imposter syndrome* (Clance & Imes, 1978). Students who have imposter syndrome might be perfectionists or have perfectionistic parents. No matter how hard they work, they will not believe that any achievement is good enough. Girls sometimes pick up messages from the culture that they are not supposed to be good at math and science and will underperform because of lack of belief in themselves. Other students might have to work very hard to learn and believe they are not smart. In reality, working hard is necessary for most of us most of the time, even if we are skilled and intelligent.

If the teacher or counselor notices a disconnect between their evaluation of the student and the student's evaluation of themself, a new look at that student might need to be taken. If the student is accurate, and the teacher/counselor is not, they need to adjust their expectations. If the student is inaccurate, the teacher/counselor will have to change the student's opinions about themself. That might mean encouraging the student to realize they have more ability than they thought they had or convincing the student to work harder in order to actually achieve an achievable skill level.

Spectrograms

Goals addressed: Critical Thinking, Decision-making, Self-Awareness, Sequencing, and Social Connection.

Space requirements: A long space from one side of the room to the other.

Teacher/Counselor participation: Caller and Coach.

Supplies suggested: When first learning how to create a spectrogram, the imaginary line could be concretized on the floor with masking tape.

A spectrogram is an imaginary line, which creates a continuum from low or zero to high or ten (or another number). The purpose of a spectrogram is to get group members to evaluate a topic, make choices, and think on their feet. They can also see where others in the group stand in relation to themself. The word spectrogram comes from spectrum (or continuum) and gram (for measurement).

Ask students to imagine a line on the floor from one end of the room to the other or, if the room is very big, from one object in the room to another. Indicate which end is low/least/zero and which is high/most/ten. Identify an object halfway between both ends.

Provide a criterion that people could have different points of view about. After a criterion is spoken, players move to the place on the line they feel best expresses their position or opinion on the topic. In a spectrogram session, usually a set of 8–15 statements or questions are posed to the group.

Helpful Hints:

- Occasionally vary which side of the room represents high and low to encourage participants to continue to think actively and make choices. You do not need to vary with every criterion, maybe after every four or five.
- Toward the beginning, mix criteria that reference the topic directly with ones relating to students in the here and now in order to warm-up their choice making.
- Do not allow students too much time for thinking about choices before moving.
- If students ask you to clarify a criterion, tell them it is up to them to interpret it (Discussions can be had about the criterion after the group moves).

Spectrograms are useful as a warm-up and as an introduction to a new or controversial topic. They can be used in drama sessions or as lead-ins to academic subjects. The group leader can see where the participants fall on the continuum and can see patterns within the group. Participants can evaluate where they stand individually on each question and also see the patterns in the class as a whole.

If you were going to teach a class about freedom of speech, you might use a list of criteria like this:

- I feel alert and awake right now.
- Eating lunch re-energized me.
- I like expressing my opinion.
- I believe everyone wants to listen to my opinions.
- The First Amendment to the Constitution states, "Congress shall make no law respecting an establishment of religion, or prohibiting the free exercise thereof; or abridging the freedom of speech, or of the press; or the right of the people peaceably to assemble, and to petition the government for a redress of grievances." How important is Freedom of Speech to you?
- Freedom of speech means I can say anything I want to about anyone at any time, even if it isn't true (agree totally to disagree totally).
- I have been told to be quiet (never-sometimes-often).
- When I was told to be quiet, my freedom of speech was taken away.
- This topic seems like an interesting one to discuss further.

Working Together

Employers want to hire people who can work with others on teams, whether they are the wait staff at a restaurant or lawyers in a firm. Most schoolwork is given to students to do individually by themselves. To work together on these assignments would require sharing ideas and answers, and in the minds of some, that would constitute cheating. Later when students are put on teams to solve a problem together, build a robot, or rehearse a play, they are usually not taught the skills needed to work as a team. I have seen group projects strike fear into the hearts of college students.

What do students need to know about working on an academic team? To begin with, an academic team is not the same as a sports team: There are not the same type of clear positions that are played. Often the group has no one designated as the leader. Typically, the teacher or counselor is functioning as the coach – from a distance. As a result, less motivated participants may take a step back and let one or two group members, who are the most responsible or the most worried about their grade, step up and do most of the work. Does this sound familiar?

The first thing that students should know about working on a team is that everyone is connected. There is no stepping back – all are needed to contribute to the group's work in some way. What one team member does or does not do effects all the other team members. Everyone does not have to do the same task, but all the tasks need to be done, and there should be a fair division of work.

The process to be followed when working in a group relates to basic executive functions as shown in Figure 3.1: Task Planning and Organization are needed to prepare for the task. Task Monitoring follows and includes the doing the task and keeping track of the steps being done in the correct sequence. Finally, Task Evaluation happens after the first draft of the task is completed to make sure the job has been done well. If the task passes the evaluation, the group is finished. If the task does not

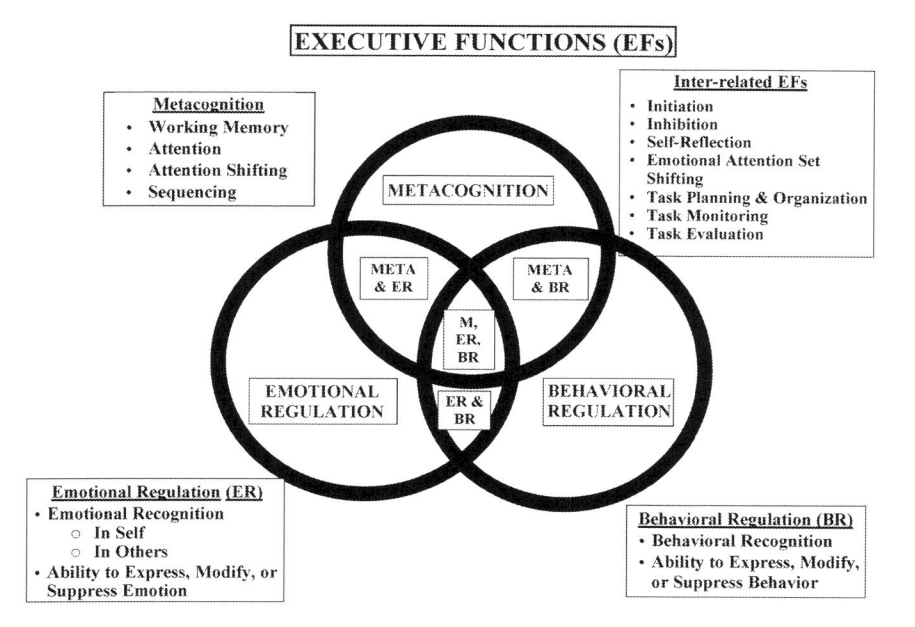

Figure 3.1 Executive Functions: Main categories with sub-functions and sub-functions that require more than one main category.

pass evaluation, group members have to figure out what went wrong and make adjustments.

These concepts can be taught through the drama games included in the section below as well as through the communication games earlier in the chapter. The first games in this section highlight the aspect of connection that all members of a team have. The later games begin incorporating planning, monitoring, and evaluation.

Elastablasts (Also Called Cooperabands Or Buddy Bands)

Goals addressed: Body Control, Boundaries, Gross Motor Skills, Problem-solving, Task Organizational Skills, and Teamwork.

Space requirements: Large open space.

Teacher/Counselor participation: Player and Coach.

Supplies needed: At least one large Elastablast Exercise Band (24 feet in diameter for 10–20 people).

Elastablasts are large bungee cords covered in soft, colorful fleece material. They are fun to play with and easy to hold onto. They create a connection between all members of a group because when one player pulls on the band, it affects everyone else holding on.

To begin with, just play around with the band. Allowing each student pull on the band and let the others hold on see how it affects them.

Try creating an ocean with calm water. Have a storm roll in and make the water rough. Then let the calm return.

Explore the different shapes you can make with the band: circles, ovals, squares, rectangles, triangles, polygons, five point stars, six point stars, etc. This would be a great exploration for a geometry lesson (see Chapter Five).

Pretend that the band is a magic carpet that everyone can use to fly to anyplace in the world. Where does the class want to go? What happens when the wind blows at different strengths? Or you get lost in a cloud? If the magic carpet is flying too low, you might have to quickly jerk it higher to avoid hitting a building or a tall mountain. You might have to jerk it lower to go through a tunnel or under an underpass. What if you are way up in the clouds and the group wants to fly lower to see something more closely? Can you glide down slowly?

Bands create a fascinating pressure to push against if students are inside them pressing out. Students who have sensory integration problems will love this! Many students with ADHD and autism spectrum disorder (ASD) need this kind of deep pressure to help them focus. You might see a big shift in behavior while using the band.

Variation: Parachutes

Goals addressed: Body Control, Boundaries, Gross Motor Skills, Problem-solving, Task Organizational Skills, and Teamwork.

Space requirements: Large open space.

Teacher/Counselor participation: Player and Coach.

Supplies needed: Large parachute and different size balls.

Parachutes create a similar type of connected team experience as Elastablasts. If you do not have access to a parachute, see if the physical education department or school occupational therapist has one you could borrow.

In addition to playing around with the parachute as described above with the Elastablast, you can put different sizes and amounts of balls on the surface. One effective team activity is having one ball that the group works together to roll around the surface of the parachute in a clockwise or counter-clockwise direction. Everyone will be able to see and feel how the others are working together (or not!).

A number of small balls can be placed on the surface of the parachute, and the class can create a popcorn popper, trying to keep the balls on the parachute and not bouncing them off.

The group can flick the parachute as high as possible, run to the center and sit down to create a big floating mushroom shape above their heads (of course, it eventually collapses all over everyone, but that is part of the fun).

There are many parachute games. I have listed two excellent books in the Reference list at the end of this chapter (Strong & LeFevre, 1996; Wilmes & Wilmes, 2000).

Scarf Ball Toss

Goals addressed: Body Control, Gross Motor Skills, Problem-solving, Task Organizational Skills, and Teamwork.

Space requirements: Large open space.

Teacher/Counselor participation: Coach.

Number of students: A minimum of 12 students (four per scarf).

Supplies needed: At least three large scarves and either a balloon or a beach ball.

This game needs to be played with at least 12 players. The corners of each scarf are held by a player and the scarves are lined up in a row with about three feet between each. A balloon or beach ball is placed on the first scarf. The first scarf holders throw the ball to the second scarf. That group works to catch the ball. The second group throws the ball to the third group, which catches the ball. The ball is then thrown scarf by scarf back to the first scarf.

If there are more players, one or more scarves can be added after the third scarf.

If your students are able to handle competition, and you have a minimum of 24 students and six scarves, Scarf Ball Toss can be played as a competitive game to see which team gets the ball to the last scarf and back to the front first.

To increase the difficulty, every other scarf on each team can be switched so that the ball has to be thrown diagonally from scarf to scarf instead of back to front.

Helpful Hint: If you decide to do diagonal scarf/ball tosses in a race, make all the scarves for each team the same color so it is clear where the ball is to be thrown.

Relay Race With No Hands

Goals addressed: Body Control, Boundaries, Generate Alternatives, Gross Motor Skills, Problem-solving, Task Organizational Skills, and Teamwork.

Space Requirements: A large space in which a relay race can be run. This might work well outside on the playground or in the gym.

Teacher/Counselor participation: Coach.

Materials needed: A ball for each team.

The group is divided into teams. Half of each team crosses to the opposite side of the room/space. Each team member finds a partner on their side. If there is an odd number on each side, send one of the single players to the other side to create a pair. If there is just one single team member without a partner, that player can work with the Coach as a referee.

Decide on an order in which the pairs on each side will cross the room. When a pair gets across, they give their ball to the next pair on the other side of the room, and that pair brings the ball back to the starting side, switch to the next pair, and so on.

Each team pair decides how they will move the ball from their side of the room to the other side of the room *without using their hands* to transport the ball. This means they must use some other part of their bodies. It does not have to be the same part on each player (like two elbows). It could be one player's elbow and the other player's hip or one player's head and the other player's back. Each pair must use a different type of carry.

At the starting signal, the first pair from each team cross the room with their ball. If the ball is dropped, that pair must go back to where they started and begin again. This means speed is not as important as working together. The next pair must use a different way to take the ball back across the room. The game continues until all the pairs have gone. The first team to get all of its pairs across the room, wins.

1776

Goals addressed: Attention, Teamwork, and Working Memory
Space requirements: Enough space to form a circle.
Teacher/Counselor participation: Player and Coach.

This is an advanced version of Elephant and Giraffe (which was in the previous chapter). The group stands in a circle facing in with one Player standing in the middle. The Center Player points to a Player in the circle and calls one of five positions: Giraffe, Elephant, Hamburger, Jello, or 1776.

- For Giraffe, the Player raises arms straight up in the air as if making the neck of a giraffe.

- For Elephant, the Player pointed to becomes the trunk of the elephant, and the Players on either side create the ears with their arms.

- For Hamburger, the Player pointed to creates a hamburger patty with arms folded in front at chest level, while the Players on either side create the bun with their arms.

- For Jello, the Player pointed to jiggles like Jello, while the Players on either side create the bowl around the Jello with their arms.

- For 1776, the Player pointed to pretends to hold the American Flag, the Player on the right pretends to play the drum, and the Player on the left pretends to play a fife, creating a reenactment of the painting "The Spirit of 1776."

The Center Player counts to ten as fast as possible immediately after announcing the position.

Helpful Hint: Show students a photo of the painting "The Spirit of 1776" so they can better visualize the image they are creating. (In the actual painting, the middle and right figures are both playing the drum, but the flag is in the center of the picture behind them, which is why the center figure holds the flag.)

The point of the game is for the Center Player to get out of the center and into the circle. When a Player makes a mistake while creating their position or does not create the position by the end of the count, they must become the Center Player, and the Player, who has been in the center, can come into the circle. If the group gets skilled at getting into position quickly, the count can be lowered to seven or five so the Center Player does not stay in the middle all the time.

Variation: Add more positions: If your class enjoys this game, they can add additional positions. For Airplane, the Player pointed to creates a pair of goggles using his/her fingers and the Players on either side create the wings of the plane. For Fish Sandwich, the Player pointed to sticks arms out forward on top of each other (creating the shape of a fish) while the Players on either side create the bun. For Volcano, the Player pointed to becomes the lava with hands raised over head, pretending to spew lava, and the Players on either side become the mountainside. The group can make up as many positions as they can remember!

Environments

Goals addressed: Improvisation, Nonverbal Communication, and Teamwork.

Space requirements: Open space for groups to plan separately and then come together to share their environments.

Teacher/Counselor participation: Coach.

Divide the class into small groups of four to six players. Each group decides on an environment somewhere in the universe to act out. It could even be a fictional place like Hogwarts School or Wonderland. Players can be people, animals, or objects in this environment. The group can present their environment using only pantomime or using dialogue and movement. If the players speak, they need to try not to say where they are.

When each group performs their environments, the audience does not verbally guess where the environment is. They must get up and join the environment, becoming a person, animal, or object in it. If they are correct, the original players will incorporate them into the scene. If they are incorrect, they have to leave the scene. After a few minutes, the Leader freezes the scene and asks the remaining audience where the scene is happening.

Helpful Hint: The Coach should check in with each group while they are planning to make sure two groups have not chosen the same environment. It is very disappointing for players when that happens. The group that would have gone second will not want to perform if they know they are duplicating something another group has just done.

This is a great beginning improvisation game to get students familiar with making up actions and words in a situation.

Museum Guard/Night At The Museum

Goals addressed: Attention, Body Control, Decision-making, Initiation, Impulse Control (Inhibition), Problem-solving, Social Skills, Spatial Awareness, and Teamwork.

Space requirements: An open space in which students can move.

Teacher/Counselor participation: Player or Coach.

Supplies needed: Set of keys on a keychain.

One person (the Coach or a Player) is the Night Guard at a museum. The rest of the players are Statues in the museum. The Guard's keys are set either at the guard station or on the floor by a chair (as if they have fallen out of the Guard's pocket). When the Guard turns away from the group, the Statues come alive. They want to escape the museum so they try to sneak up and steal the keys. Each time the Guard turns to face them, the Statues must freeze and not move. If the Guard sees any movement, the observed Statue must go back to their original starting point. Once one of the Statues has the keys, the group must work together to get the keys to the exit and unlock the door to the museum so they can escape. When Guard realizes that the keys are gone, a search for them begins. The Statues must be sure that the Guard cannot see the keys, or the Guard will take the keys back to the guard station, and the Statues will have to steal them again.

This is a version of Red Light/Green Light, but involves more strategy, characterization, teamwork, and excitement. If your group has difficulty playing Night Guard, you could work with them on Red Light/Green Light first and build up to Night Guard.

A simpler version for beginning students: Statues do not have to steal anything or work as a team, they can just focus on moving whenever the guard is not looking at them and freeze when the guard turns and can see them.

Machines

Goals addressed: Body Control, Boundaries, Generate Alternatives, Initiation, Problem-solving, Sequencing, and Teamwork.

Space requirements: A large enough space for the group to create a moving statue.

Teacher/Counselor participation: Coach and Player.

The group's goal is to create a "Machine," comprised of people who act as the machine's moving parts and sounds. The initial instructions might be:

> A machine is made up of many parts. One part makes another part move, and it makes another part move, and that makes another part move, and so on, until the machine does whatever its job is. The parts do the same thing, again and again and again.
>
> [If you have a simple toy or object, you can demonstrate that concept, or you can set up three or four students to demonstrate.] We are going to build a machine, and each of you will be a part in the machine. You will each think of one movement and one sound to use.

Helpful Hint: While parts of a real machine touch, parts in a drama machine do not. This makes it a safe game for players who are tactilely defensive.

Helpful Hint: Make sure the first players to start pick a movement that can be repeated again and again without the players becoming exhausted. For instance, deep knee bends are not a great movement choice to start a machine.

There are a number of variations of this game. Start with a version that you think your students will understand and enjoy the most.

Abstract machine: One person starts the machine with a sound and movement, then another joins in relationship to the sound and movement that the first has made. Other members of the group join one by one, adding on to another part until the machine is complete. They can add on to any of the parts in any direction. The machine might end up in a line, a circle, or a big clump. You can give directions to the machine to speed up or slow down. You can also tell it to "Freeze!" Ask the machine parts what they think they made and what they would like to name their machine.

Real machine: Students could decide on a real machine to build or pick the name of a real machine from a hat. Machine groups work best if there are at least five or six members so there will be enough moving parts. The group can be larger if students can handle working together as a large team without conflict.

Options for creating the machine:

- The group can co-design the machine and volunteer for the parts they want to be.

- One person in the group can be assigned to be the "director" of the machine. That person designs it and decides who will do what part.

- If the group is advanced, they could improvisationally create the machine without discussing the design. This requires everyone to carefully watch each other and step in to fill the obvious gaps in the machine.

Invented Machine: Each group decides on a machine that does not exist, yet would solve an important problem. If students have difficulty deciding on an idea, the Coach could make up some ideas for groups to pick. Examples of inventions could be a Homework Machine, a Super Duper Morning Alarm Clock, a Dressing Machine, a Self-Cleaning Bedroom, a Magic Erasing White Board, etc.

Helpful Hint: For a game in which imagination is the rule, I always tell my students that in drama the rules of physics do not apply, so they will not censure themselves. If you are a science teacher, you might not want to say that, and I understand; however, the idea is to get students to "think outside of the box."

Hot Chocolate River

Goals addressed: Body Control, Generate Alternatives, Problem-solving, Task Organizational Skills, and Teamwork

Space requirements: Large space in which one long and wide "river" can be created with banks on both sides.

Teacher/Counselor participation: Coach.

Materials needed: Masking tape, small carpet squares, or mats.

Use tape on the floor to indicate the two banks of a wide river. Divide the class into small teams (about four players in each). Each team must cross the Hot Chocolate River using their marshmallows (carpet squares/mats). You probably want to use one less marshmallow than team players.

Problem to solve: At least one foot must be kept on a marshmallow at all times, or it will float away in the river. There are not enough marshmallows to get across the river without re-using them. A few players who are not on the crossing team will need to be part of the river so if a member of the group forgets and takes a foot off a marshmallow, the river people take it away. The goal is to cross the river with the most marshmallows left.

Allow the group to work through the problem. If they lose their marshmallows, they will have to go back to the bank they started from and try again. They can have all their starting marshmallows back each time they attempt to solve the problem anew.

References

Beal, D. (2014, March 29). *Games for the classroom* {Conference session]. Theatre in Our Schools American Alliance of Theatre in Education, Seattle, WA, United States.

Cattanach, A. (1992). *Drama for people with special needs*. Drama Book Publishers.

Clance, N., & Imes, S. (1978). The imposter phenomenon in high achieving women: Dynamics and therapeutic intervention. *Psychotherapy: Theory, Research, and Practice, 15*(3), pp. 241–247.

Kruger, J., & Dunning, D. (1999). Unskilled and unaware of it: How difficulties in recognizing one's own incompetence lead to inflated self-assessments. *Journal of Personality and Social Psychology 77*(6), 1121–1134.

Lessac, A. (1967). *The use and training of the human voice: A practical approach to speech and voice dynamics*. Drama Book Specialists.

Strong, T., & LeFevre, D. (1996). *Parachute games*, Human Kinetics. (with DVD).

Wilmes, L., & Wilmes, D. (2000). *Parachute play: For indoor and outdoor fun*. Building Blocks.

Developing Improvisation Skills

Once students have increased their abilities to pay attention, listen to and communicate with each other, and work together, they are ready to learn how to improvise. Some of the games and experiments that were done in Chapters Two and Three required basic improvisational acting. This chapter focuses squarely on the rules of improvisation. Improvising scenes allows students to explore social-emotional issues, develop empathy, and improve their flexibility and spontaneity. Improvising can also help students learn about curricular subjects (more on that in Chapter Five). Ultimately, students' self-discipline, confidence, and respect for fellow students will grow.

Empathy

Empathy helps us understand other people – what they think and what they feel – without losing the sense of ourselves. In other words, empathy allows one person in conversation or connection with another to understand the other's perspective on the world. When a person has developed their empathy, they can simulate in their body what another is feeling, while at the same time not getting confused about which thoughts or feelings belong to whom. There are two different types of empathy: Cognitive empathy (thoughts) and affective empathy (emotions). They are processed through different systems in the brain.

Empathy motivates prosocial behaviors. It is involved in social understanding, compassion, caring, cooperation, sharing, donating, and other forms of altruism. Empathy stimulates friendships and allows us to keep friends once they are made, because we can learn about and appreciate our friends' needs. Without empathy we would not be able to live in social groups nor – would we be able to successfully negotiate solutions to problems that inevitably develop between each other.

Young children are egocentric. At birth, they have the ability to connect with the adults around them, but they are unable to differentiate between "me" and "not me." As they grow, depending on the interactions they have with their parents and other people in their lives, they usually begin to understand that they are not the center of the universe and not all people think and feel exactly as they do: Different people have different ideas, feelings, and desires. The more sheltered or more catered to children are, the more they remain egocentric. The more they learn how to appropriately connect and interact with others, the more empathy they develop.

Empathy leads to success in life at home, at school, and at work. It is more important for the lasting of a romantic relationship than physical attraction. It allows people to become successful and loving parents. Lack of empathy creates problems. Children who are lower in empathy skills demonstrate more overtly aggressive behaviors, misunderstand the social cues of the people around them, and end up in trouble for fighting, stealing, and other anti-social behaviors.

There are many ways to develop empathy. Psychologists suggest reading fiction to get into the minds of other characters, doing compassion-based mindfulness meditation, working in cooperative groups, and intellectually "putting yourself into others' shoes." However, the one type of intervention that has worked most successfully in the vast majority of empathy trainings for children and adults is *role-play* (Lanzoni, 2018). Role-play is another name for improvisation. Participants act out roles different from themselves, and fictional situations are dramatically improvised. Through that process, the viewpoint of the role taken on is understood viscerally. This activates affective empathy. Discussions after scenes take the embodied learning of the improvisation and allow words to be found to describe it, making them available to cognitive understanding. As a result, cognitive empathy develops.

In her book *The Empathy Effect* (2018) Helen Riess lays out the keys to developing empathy in her E.M.P.A.T.H.Y. teaching program. E is for eye contact, M is for Muscles of Facial Expression, P is for Posture, A is for Affect, T is for Tone of Voice, H is for Hearing the Whole Person, and Y is for Your Response. As you read the rest of the chapter on how to do improvisation, pay attention to how all of these aspects of developing empathy are involved in the rules of improvisation and in most of the games in this book.

The Rules of Improvisation

Life is improvised. Although we have routine expressions we frequently use for many of the common occasions we interact with others, most of what we say is made up on the spot. The words coming out of our mouths are directly related to what is going on at the moment. True, when people reminisce, they often develop a ritual story that is repeated in a very similar manner from telling to telling, but most of the time we are not reminiscing, we are in action.

Improvisation is an American theatre phenomenon, created by social worker and drama teacher Viola Spolin from the 1920s to 1960s and developed further by her son Paul Sills and his colleagues at the Second City Theatre Company in the late 50s through the 60s (Wasson, 2017). Since then, improvisation as an art form has grown and spread to the rest of the world. The way Spolin taught improvisation was to use theatre games (see Chapters Two and Three) to help participants learn how to work with each other, create an ensemble, trust their impulses, and respond honestly to the others in the group. She saw it as a way to create community, trust, and equality between people and to free people to be themselves (Wasson, 2017).

Not all improvisation is meant to be humorous. Second City Theatre shows are comedies because that is what audiences will pay to see; they want to be entertained. Many other theatre and non-theatre groups have employed improvisation for developing characters in plays, exploring social and psychological issues in an embodied way, training employees in people skills, and helping people increase their creativity, flexibility, and spontaneity. Harold Ramis[1], a company member of Second City in the 70s and 80s, has said, "What Second City taught me was how to play well with others" in reference to all the training he had in improvisation and theatre games (Patinkin, 2000, p. 191).

While you will find the following rules for improvisation in many books, my specific sources (which I recommend) are *Lessons from the Second City, Yes, and: How Improvisation Reverses "No, but" Thinking and Improves Creativity and Collaboration* (Leonard & Yorton, 2015), and *Applied Improvisation: Leading, Collaborating, and Creating Beyond Theatre* (Dudeck & McClure, 2018).

Yes, and …

There are not many rules for improvisation, but a few are canon. The most important is the rule of "Yes, and … " In any improvisational interaction, the first actor makes an "offer," saying or doing something that expresses a problem they are having or what they are feeling or where they are. The second actor responds by accepting that offer and building on it. In the beginning, while students are learning improvisation, they often literally say, "Yes, and …" each time they start a line to remind themselves that their job is agreeing and building. The structure of an improvised scene is like a game of tennis. One actor makes an offer, the other actor accepts it and makes an offer back to the first actor, and so on.

Improvisers are not supposed to say (or perform), "No, but …" or "Maybe, but …" or even "Yes, but …" That is referred to as "blocking the offer" of the other actor. Blocking stops the forward movement of a scene and takes the actors right back to square one. The second actor takes power away from the first actor if an offer is rejected. That creates one active and one passive actor. In this situation, nothing constructive can develop.

Another objective of "Yes, and …" is to jointly flesh out the details of the dramatic situation, because most often improvised scenes are not pre-planned, and no one knows exactly what is going to happen. The actors may have been told who they are and where they are, but most of the details need to be created through the scene. The actors work together to develop the scene by negotiating the meaning as they go.

The beginning of an improvisation scene using "Yes, and …" might go like this:

ONE: (*holding jaw in hands and moaning in pain*) Oh … Oh …!
TWO: Toothache?

ONE: (*nodding*) The worst!
TWO: When was the last time you went to the dentist?

ONE: (*shrugs*) I don't know …
TWO: Hmmm … You could have an abscess in that tooth.

ONE: (*moans despondently*) Ohhhhhh …
TWO: Let me take a look!

ONE: (*considering it*) Ohhhh???
TWO: I could see if it's red and swollen back there.

ONE: (*thinking it's a good idea*) Ohhhh!

TWO: Come over here where there's more light … open your mouth …

ONE: (*It's really hard to open, but ONE tries.*) Ahhhhh …

TWO: That's right, open your mouth … just a little bit more … turn your head, and … (*Pause.*) Hmmmm! … Hmmm! It's really dark in there! Hold on, I'll go get a flashlight. (*TWO crosses to the cupboard.*)

ONE: (*closes mouth*) Oh.

As soon as Two finds that flashlight, the scene is bound to continue.

Now let's analyze this structure, because the "Yes, ands" were acted out, but not literally said.

ONE: (*holding hands around head and moaning in pain*) Oh … Oh …!
One makes an offer, but doesn't identify exactly what is wrong.

TWO: Toothache?
Two accepts the offer and suggests (offers back) that One has a toothache. One may not have thought about having a toothache, instead One may have thought about having a headache, being punched in the face, or something else, but …

ONE: (*nodding*) The worst!
By saying "The worst!" One accepts Two's offer, and the scene is off to a strong start.

TWO: When was the last time you went to the dentist?
Two generously offers One the opportunity to add some specifics about the situation instead of making all the choices for the scene, but …

ONE: (*shrugs*) I don't know …
One has accepted the toothache so completely that the pain makes it hard to think.

TWO: Hmmm … You could have an abscess in that tooth.
Two makes another offer.

ONE: (*moans despondently*) Ohhhhhh …
One is now playing the scene for all's it's worth (maybe the audience has started laughing as they recognize the situation, having been in One's situation before.)

TWO: Hey! Let me take a look!
Two accepts the job of "straight man" or "comic foil."[2]

ONE: (*considering it*) Ohhhh???

One has not said, "No," and is providing information on how much it hurts.

TWO: I could see if it's red and swollen back there.

Two is accepting that offer and offering back help. One can't look into their own mouth!.

ONE: (*thinking it's a good idea*) Ohhhh!

One accepts that offer.

TWO: Come over here where there's more light … open your mouth …

Two accepts One's offer and sets up the at-home mouth examination.

ONE: (*It's really hard to open mouth, but ONE tries.*) Ahhhhh …

One accepts the examination and tries to comply, but it's painful.

TWO: That's right, open your mouth … just a little bit more…turn your head, and … Hmmm! … Hmmm! It's really dark in there! Hold on, I'll go get a flashlight.

Two is having a problem seeing anything and figures out a way to solve the problem.

ONE: (*closes mouth*) Oh.

One accepts Two's offer to wait while Two is searching for the flashlight.

Both actors had *obstacles* to deal within this scene. Obstacles are good; in fact, they are necessary in drama. Obstacles give the actors something to overcome, and that struggle to overcome the obstacles is the essence of drama. It makes a scene interesting to the actors and the audience. Actor One could only open his mouth a little bit, and Actor Two could not see inside Actor One's mouth because it was too dark in there, but those obstacles did not stop the action. The actors kept "Yes, anding …" trying new actions to solve the problem. Even in those moments when One momentarily considers resisting Two's help, One still allows the scene to move forward with a "Yes, and … "

Here's a version of the same situation in which the actors are not "Yes, anding …" each other.

ONE: (*holding hands on head and moaning in pain*) Oh … Oh …!

TWO: Stop it! I can't concentrate on my book!

ONE: (*continues moaning in pain*) Oh … Oh …!

TWO: If you are going to be over-dramatic, I'm going to leave. (*Gets up and leaves the room*).

At this point, the scene ends. The two actors are not working together. Similar to that conversation in Chapter Three in the Conversation Practice that never got off the ground, the two characters were not listening to each other.

Listening is Essential

Improvisers should make a habit of *deeply listening* to each other. Deep listening is another way of saying, *active* or *responsive listening*. It is listening to the other person's body language, tone of voice, emotions, and even eyes, in addition to listening to the words. If an actor is only listening shallowly to a partner, that means the actor is preoccupied or thinking about what to say next. They will not really know what their partner said or meant. This is true in real life, as well. Too many people miscommunicate through lack of deep listening. In an improvised scene, an offer not deeply listened to might be negated instead of accepted. And … the scene will come to a dead end.

There have already been a number of listening exercises that your students have practiced by the time you get to this chapter. By now they should be primed for this rule. If not, more listening practice is in order.

Commit!

The actor must commit 100% to the scene, even if it feels silly or difficult. If all the actors are committed, they will be working together and helping each other. They won't be second-guessing themselves or their partner. They won't be holding back or being hesitant about making a choice. They will find a way to bring the scene to life together.

Everything is Co-Created

In the world of improvisation there are no stars. The actors are all members of the *ensemble*. Ensemble is a word that comes from French, meaning "at the same time" or "together." Ensemble acting relies on actors working together toward the same goal of telling a story to the audience. An improvisational ensemble functions by reason of equality and respect. They all are well aware of how difficult it is to create something out of nothing. No one knows who will come up with the next best, greatest idea for the scene. As a result, everyone keeps their minds open and keeps listening to and working with everyone else. And "Yes, anding" them.

Everything is Co-Created is related to the next two rules: Follow the Follower and Make Your Partner Look Good.

Follow the Follower

Follow the Follower means any improviser can use their unique expertise and perspective on life to suggest ways to solve problems. No one is more of an expert than anyone else. The playing field is level. Everyone brings their own set of wisdom to improvisation. We all need to be willing to listen to everyone else and give them the benefit of the "Yes, and ..." doubt.

Make Your Partner Look Good

As in all improvisational ensembles, each actor puts focus on the other and is responsible for providing whatever help the other needs in that moment to move the scene forward. No thought is given to future parts of the scene or what you want to make happen ultimately. You both will know what to do when you get there. No thought is put on making oneself look good. This relates back to deep listening and working as an ensemble.

Authenticity

Improvisation is based on how people really think and feel. Sometimes improvisational acting is exaggerated, but it is always based in reality. If two students are acting out a scene about a problem, they can't have Superman fly in at the last minute to solve the problem. The characters in the scene must solve the problem themselves without superpowers.[3] This also means not hiding the things that are usually politely hidden in daily life, but letting them come out by the end of the scene. Often those issues are not only the meat of the scene, but also what needs to be worked through by the characters for a better outcome.

Of course, in a school environment, this means expressing that authenticity must be done within good taste. There are certain topics, behaviors, and words that most likely are out of bounds in your classroom, but which might appear on stage at Second City or on *Saturday Night Live*. The teacher needs to take the responsibility for selecting the situations for the improvisations and the characters that will be involved, especially while students are learning how to improv. This selection of situation and characters scaffolds the direction for the dramatic explorations.

The teacher absolutely must feel empowered to set the rules and the boundaries for behavior when students are improvising. If students start to get silly, scatological, gross, or outrageous in the middle of a scene, the teacher can say: "That choice was inappropriate [or unbelievable or inauthentic], let's rewind to _____ [a previous moment in the scene] and take it from there."

Using the words "not realistic" instead of "inappropriate," can prompt an argument from students who point to a TV show or a movie where it [whatever action was tried] was done. To explore real-life problems like bullying, cheating, dealing with someone unpleasant, or resolving a conflict, students need to remain authentic, no matter how much easier it might be to take a shortcut.

Talking about authenticity brings us to honesty and openly accepting failure.

Failure Happens

Improv actors do not have to worry about making a mistake – they *know* they will make them. There is no point in trying to hide a mistake – it is right there out in the open. Anyone watching the scene is going to see it; anyone in the scene is going to feel it. But that's OK, because mistakes are how we learn! In fact, failure is a big part of authenticity.

If something does not quite work in a scene, the scene can be replayed a different way. In life there are very few do-overs, but improvisation is not real life! In improv there *are* do-overs! What freedom! In fact, improvising something the wrong way can be very useful to do the first time a scene is improvised, as the baseline to exploring more successful ways. Solve the problem in the scene the wrong way and take that option off the table! Then explore other ways to solve the problem.

Some of those attempts may end in failure, too, but others may end in wonderful, glorious success.

Being willing to fail can be very freeing! One of the beautiful aspects of exploring life through drama is there may be some wrong answers, but there are many more right ones! And that variety of right answers leads us in many directions that result in different consequences.

In case you have very driven, perfectionistic students, who do not like to make mistakes, there are a few drama exercises you can do to loosen them up and make failure in a scene not something to be feared.

Failure Celebration

Goals addressed: Emotional Tolerance, Opposite Action Skills, Permission to Fail, and Stress Management Skills.

Space requirements: Students sit in a circle facing each other.

Teacher participation: Participant.

All students tell a story about a time they failed (however, please begin by requesting that they not tell their most traumatic or embarrassing failure, just a simple, everyday one). After each story is told, instead of criticism, the entire class cheers and celebrates the failure.

Failure Vaccination

Goals addressed: Emotional Tolerance, Opposite Action Skills, Permission to Fail, and Stress Management Skills.

Space requirements: Open space where students can move around.

Teacher participation: Coach.

The participants walk around the room, and each time they pass someone, they say, "I failed!" with great joy, and the person they pass congratulates them and says with great joy, "I failed, too!"

The Terrible Magician (by Amanda Sasser)

Goals addressed: Emotional Tolerance, Opposite Action Skills, Permission to Fail, and Stress Management Skills.

Space requirements: Open space with students standing in a circle.

Teacher participation: Player and coach.

Supplies required: Depending on the group, the Terrible Magician can pantomime magic tricks or there could be a box with suggestions of bad magic tricks and a selection of props that might be used in magic, such as a few scarves, a deck of cards, a hat, a bunny puppet, etc.

One by one, going around the circle counterclockwise, each player pretends to be a Magician doing their most famous trick. The person to their right acts as their assistant. However, the trick fails horribly (in whatever way the Magician chooses). The Assistant, then, must find a way to complement the Magician on something they did that was "brilliant." Everyone applauds. The Assistant then becomes the Magician, and the tricks continue around the circle.

Helpful Hint: If the teacher goes first, the students will be able to use them for a model of what to do.

Helpful Hint: Make sure your Magicians are not doing something that puts themselves, their Assistants, or anyone else in the circle in danger!

Setting Up an Improvisational Scene

Space Concerns

Depending on the space you have to work in, three options are shared below as possible ways to arrange audience members and actors. The best in terms of the audience seeing everything is the last one; however, in case that option would be hard to create in your space, the other two options are offered as alternates. I have pointed out the difficulties that the first and second options have in terms of audience members' sightlines. Perhaps there are ideas for working around those difficulties in your space.

Option One

Use a large circle of chairs as the audience area. Volunteer actors improvise short scenes in the middle of the circle (the acting area). Once the acting is done, the actors go back and sit in their seats in the circle.

The drawbacks with this set up is that in a circle, at least one actor will have his or her back to one area of the circle at any given time. Those audience members will not be able to see that actor's face and, if the actor is soft spoken, may not be able to hear what is being said clearly. Sometimes in this configuration, an actor's body can block the other actors' bodies from certain areas of the circle. Audience members who have difficulty seeing or hearing will have difficulty paying attention to the scene.

Option Two

A horseshoe formation could be created instead of a circle. The acting area would be put at the open end of the horseshoe. Most students will be able to see and hear all the actors. However, the students seated near the open ends of the horseshoe may have a little difficulty seeing actors on the opposite end of the opening.

Option Three

A third space option is to create an open acting area on one side of the room and have the audience in chairs facing the acting area. The acting area could be designated by masking tape on the floor so the actors clearly know where their boundaries are. The acting area does not need to be huge, but should have enough space for students to set up a simple location for the scene (living room, restaurant, bus stop) with chairs and still have room to move. This configuration will provide the best sightlines to the audience members.

Enroling Actors in an Improvisational Scene

As mentioned earlier, when creating improv scenes with students, the teacher should take the lead in choosing the topic, the situation, and the basic characters. Actors can be given more choices later on, but they will need a clear structure as they learn how to improvise together. The teacher first talks about the issue to be explored that day (it could be bullying, sharing, making a friend, etc.). There might be a preparatory game, a spectrogram, or a class discussion to engage students in the topic. Then the teacher presents the situation to be acted out and asks for volunteers to fill those roles.

Keep the number of characters involved in a scene small, so it does not get chaotic. The actors need to be able to concentrate, and audience members who have difficulty attenuating need to know where to focus. It is often useful to make the characters in your scenario non-gender specific so anyone interested in the scene can volunteer for a role. For instance, ask for students to play two siblings and a parent, rather than a brother, a sister, and a mother.

When the actors get to the acting area, ask them to set up the space in which the scene takes place. If it is a living room, they might choose to create a couch from two or three chairs put next to each other and use a single chair for an armchair. All the walls and furniture do not need to be represented, just the places people need to sit. Together determine where the entrances are. If there is an important prop or piece of furniture that will be needed in the scene, the placement for this also needs to be chosen, especially if it is mimed. This preparation allows the actors to clearly communicate with each other. For example, if the scene starts with both siblings watching TV and fighting over the remote control, where the TV (which may be invisible) is located will be important information for all the actors. If the actors have not agreed on this and place it in different spots, the audience will become confused.

Next, briefly interview each actor as the character they are playing. This helps clarify what they are doing and the point of view of their character in relation to the other characters, the obstacles in the scene or the conflict being explored. To keep students' personal identities separate from their characters' personalities, ask actors to pick a name different from their own (and probably different from any other students in the class so no confusion arises that maybe the actor is portraying or mocking that person in the scene).

All improvisational scenes need to remain fictional in order to keep private issues out of the role play. This helps actors avoid inadvertently revealing personal information that may be inappropriate to disclose in front of the whole class. For instance, suppose Quincy's real-life family has recently been evicted from their apartment. Revealing that information by mistake could be very embarrassing to Quincy, even if he revealed it himself. Using fictional names also frees actors to make choices that are different from the ones they, themselves, might make in this situation, allowing them to experience new perspectives and options for action.

An excellent resource about exploring real life situations through fictional means can be found in *Sociodrama: Who's in Your Shoes?* by Patricia Sternberg and Antonina Garcia (2000).

The brief interviews help the actors make choices about how to approach the scene. Questions might relate to the age of the character, what the character's relationship is the other character(s), what the character wants, and what their motivation is. The actors needs enough details about their characters to know how to play the scene. Most importantly, the actors need a clear understanding of their goals, obstacles, and their motivations (why they want or need to overcome the obstacle in order to achieve their goal). Through the interviews, the actors also become aware of what the other characters are focused on and how they are either working with them or against them in the scene.

Once actors have been interviewed, have them take their opening positions in the acting area and briefly review the situation for them and the audience: The obstacle or conflict the characters are faced with and their current location. Then start the scene off by saying, "Action," "Start," or "Curtain."

Guiding the Scene

As the scene moves forward, the action may develop fine on its own. If so, fabulous! However, if the actors get stuck, the teacher can step in and side coach to help them get unstuck.

One way to do this is to ask the actors to freeze. If they are not listening to each other, the teacher could ask, "Are you listening to each other?" or "Are you remembering to respond to offers with 'Yes, and … '?" The teacher could also make a statement like, "Remember to make an offer and accept the offer in some way." The actors can be reanimated by the teacher saying, "Action" again.

Another way to side coach a stuck scene (one that is not going anywhere) is to tell the actors to freeze. Then ask one of the stuck actors to talk about what his character is thinking and feeling right now in the scene. If the actor can do that, the teacher can then ask, "What do you want to do next?" When the actor can verbalize an action that makes sense, say, "Then when we start the scene again, go ahead and try that." The teacher moves out of the acting area and says, "Action."

Usually, getting one actor to try something new will get the scene going again. If both actors are stuck, both could be asked to verbalize what they are thinking and feeling, why they are stuck, and/or what they would like to try next. When side coaching happens, the teacher is talking with the actors, not the characters, so the characters "don't know" what's going to happen when the scene starts again.

If the situation in the scene has become a little heated between the characters, or if one is being intimidated by the other, the teacher can freeze the scene and take one of the actors on a "walk and talk." This is a short, leisurely walk around the stage area where the teacher says, "I can tell that you are not sure what to do next. Why don't you talk a bit about what your character is feeling (or what your character wants to have happen)?" Allow the actor to process what is going on and guide them back to the place they started from. If both actors seem to be stuck, the teacher could take the second actor on a "walk and talk." In either case, getting an actor out of the scene in which their character is stuck will often allow them to get a new idea in order to take a different tack on the situation.

Ending the Scene

Sometimes scenes come to a clear and obvious conclusion. The teacher can reinforce this end by saying, "Curtain" or "End Scene" at that moment. Students will clearly feel they made the right choice by ending the scene when they did.

Other times, for a variety of reasons, a scene may go on and on. To get actors to bring an "endless" scene to a close, the teacher can say, "Now, find an end to this scene." Often, the actors did want to end the scene, but were not sure how to do it. Being directed to find an end, allows that to become their focus instead of developing the situation more.

If actors do not want to stop acting because they are enjoying being on stage, sometimes the teacher must step in and end the scene. This can be done with the words "Cut," "Scene," or "Curtain." Say something like, "This is the perfect place to stop and discuss what is happening in this scene!" so that the actors do not feel like they were doing something wrong.

Allow your actors to take a bow at the end of their scene, if they want to.

Discussing the Scene

After the scene, actors can remain in their characters to be interviewed by the class. This allows the audience to explore more deeply what happened in the scene from each character's point of view. If this would be useful, have the actors sit in the stage area as their character would.

Suppose in the scene a brother and sister would not share the TV remote, and their mother came into the room, took away the remote, and turned off the TV. The teacher might start the character interviews with a statement that summarizes the scene, "We saw two siblings who would not compromise on which TV show to watch. Does anyone have any questions for the characters to find out more about this situation?" It helps if the teacher models the type of questions to ask the characters. The teacher could ask the mother, "Mom, what were you feeling when you grabbed the remote away?" "Were there any other actions you could have taken?" Actors will have an easier time staying in their character, if you use their character names.

Once the interviews with the characters are done, they can "shake off their characters" (derole) and go back into their seats in the audience. The discussion can become more general about the theme of the scene. The teacher might ask a few open-ended questions, then focus the topic on important points by asking a few close-ended ones, and finally return to open-ended questions about how the situation or conflict related to real life. "Have you experienced anything like the characters in that scene? What did you do?" "How could a situation like that be handled in a better/ different way?"

In the case of the scene with the TV remote, the teacher might ask start with open-ended questions like this:

"Why do you think Bill and Jane were so stubborn?"
"Why do you think their mother was so frustrated when she came into the room?"

And move to close-ended questions like this:

"Do you think the problem between Bill and Jane was resolved?"
"Do you think this will happen again?"

And finally move to open-ended questions again:

"What happens when people won't negotiate with each other?"
"How do you think people could be encouraged to be more flexible?"

The students may come up with a few wonderful suggestions for Bill and Jane to try in order to work out their conflict. If that happens, the same actors could replay the scene and put one of the new suggestions into practice. If you want to involve more students in acting, three different people could be asked to play out the new version of the scene.

In addition, or as an alternative to replaying the scene, a new situation with new characters could be created in which the same type of conflict was played out using the insights that students discovered in the first scene. Doing this could help students who have difficulty generalizing knowledge from one situation to another. They could see how the two situations had important aspects in common and how information could be transferred from one experience to another. Exploring a new situation may also help rigid actors, who have difficulty bringing new actions to the old situation, implement the new behavior suggestions.

Deroling

As mentioned in Chapter One, it is important to always derole actors after a scene. The more intense and exciting the scene and the more emotions that are expressed, the more the actors will need to "take off" the characters they have just played. Deroling prevents students from carrying an intense emotion into the rest of the day and projecting it onto other students or situations.

In addition to the deroling suggestions made in Chapter One, the third space option of setting up well-defined acting and audience areas can help actors derole. Make it clear to students that when actors are in the acting area, they are enroled in their characters. After the scene, when they move back into the audience area, they are no longer actors and are again themselves. The first few times the scenes are presented, the teacher can reinforce this change from character to person by saying, "And now as you cross the line of the acting area into the audience, you leave your character on the stage and move back to being yourself."

Learning to Improvise

Games to Practice Improv Techniques

Yes, And …

Goals addressed: Cognitive Flexibility, Decision-making, Generating Alternatives, Improvisation Skills, Initiation, Inhibition (Impulse Control), Listening Skills, Problem-solving, Social Skills, and Teamwork.

Space requirements: This could be done with students sitting next to each other at their desks.

Teacher participation: Coach.

Practice in pairs: The group divides into pairs. They decide who will be the Offer Maker and who will be the Offer Receiver. The pairs create several short dialogues with the Offer Maker suggesting something enjoyable for the pair to do together.

In the first round the Offer Receiver responds by saying, "No." This dialogue will not last long as the Offer Receiver has blocked the offer. Have them attempt to create a dialogue several times. Once or twice reverse roles so both students have the experience of being the actor who is blocked and being the blocking actor. Discuss this experience with the group. How did it feel to make an offer and have it rejected? How did it feel when *all* the offers were repeatedly rejected? How did it feel to block the offers? Would this have been an interesting scene to watch? Do you think any problems would have been solved?

In round two have the pairs create a short dialogue with the same offer, but with the Offer Receiver responding by saying, "Yes, but …" and coming up with a reason why the offer will not work. "Yes, but …" is really a "No" response in disguise. The dialogue will not last long and may be more frustrating for the Offer Maker than the first dialogue was. Discuss this with the group.

In the last round, have the pairs create a short dialogue with the same offer, but with the Offer Receiver saying, "Yes, and …," adding to the offer by building on what the two could do together. The Offer Maker responds, "Yes, and …" builds on the offer and continues. A real dialogue will develop as the pair makes their plans. Discuss the difference between blocking an offer and accepting an offer.

Yes, And … Scenes

Goals addressed: Cognitive Flexibility, Decision Making, Generating Alternatives, Improvisation Skills, Initiation, Inhibition (Impulse Control), Listening Skills, Problem-solving, Social Skills, and Teamwork.

Space requirements: Options: Big Circle, Horseshoe, or Acting Area/Audience set up.

Teacher participation: Coach.

Practice "Yes, and …" by creating a scene with two or more players in which no one can block any offer. Each actor must accept all offers and build on them. As the actors continue making offers, the group leader may need to help end the scene at a moment that is particularly effective. (Beginning improvisers often do not know when or how to end scenes, and some love acting so much that they do not want to stop.)

Helpful Hint: If students start being silly with their offers, the teacher can stop the scene by saying "Freeze!" (Freezing was practiced earlier, so students should be able to stop on command.) Make a few side-coaching comments to get the scene back on track.

Yes, And … Storytelling

Goals addressed: Cognitive Flexibility, Decision Making, Generating Alternatives, Improvisation Skills, Initiation, Inhibition (Impulse Control), Listening Skills, Problem-solving, Sequencing, Social Skills, Teamwork, and Working Memory.

Space requirement: Open space for a large circle.

Teacher participation: Participant and Coach.

The group stands or sits in a circle. One person starts a story. The person on the right or left of the First Storyteller very enthusiastically says, "Yes, and …" adds to the story. The next storyteller very enthusiastically says, "Yes, and …" adds to the story until the group has gotten all the way around the circle and ended the story.

The enthusiastic "Yes, and …" underlines the importance of adding to and building on a group created story, as opposed to negating a twist someone added. It also adds a tiny sense of wonder and excitement to the creative process of story making.

Corridors, Part I (Belt & Stockley, 1989)

Goals addressed: Cognitive Flexibility, Improvisation Skills, Initiation, Listening Skills, Teamwork, and Turn-taking.

Space requirements: Long enough space for students to create two lines facing each other with space in the middle.

Teacher participation: Coach.

Students line up in two lines facing each other with space between the lines. Name the lines A and B. Actors are partnered with the person in line facing them. Line A actors will think of an offer that endows their partner in Line B with a character and situation. For example, if Actor A says, "Wait until I tell Mom what you did!" it is obvious that A is a sibling of B and that B did something naughty. Actor B's response to the offer will set the scene a little more. Actor A accepts that offer and "ends" the short scene with a concluding line.

Continue down the line with each pair interacting. Then switch which side makes the first offer, so both lines have the opportunity to initiate the first offer and end the interaction.

Helpful Hint: Sometimes it is difficult for actors to stay focused on who their partner in the opposite line is. Before beginning, have each partner point directly to the other and say the partner's name or step forward and high-five their partner, staying in place long enough for the leader to make sure no one has been left out.

Helpful Hint: If actors have difficulty coming up with a first line to make an offer, the teacher could write down a number of possible first line offers and let students pick one.

Discussion: Ask if the actors were accepting offers or if any of the offers were blocked. If a line was blocked, why was it a block? (Sometimes beginning improvisers have difficulty understanding the difference between a blocked offer and a complication to a scene.)

Corridors, Part 2 (Belt & Stockley, 1989)

Goals addressed: Cognitive Flexibility, Improvisation Skills, Initiation, Listening Skills, Problem-solving, Teamwork, and Turn-taking.

Space requirements: Long enough space for students to create two lines facing each other with space in the middle.

Teacher participation: Coach.

Students line up in two lines facing each other with space between the lines. Name the lines A and B. Actors are partnered with the person in line facing them. Line A actors think of an offer that endows their partner in Line B with a character and situation. Allow the scene to go on longer until it comes to a logical ending. Try to encourage actors to keep the scenes relatively short because everyone is waiting in line for their turn!

Optional set up: Instead of having students in line, assign partners and have each pair get up and create their short scene.

Discussion: Ask if the actors were accepting offers or if any of the offers were blocked. If a line was blocked, why was it a block? (Sometimes beginning improvisers have difficulty understanding the difference between a blocked offer and a complication to a scene.)

It's Tuesday (Johnstone, 1981, p. 102)

Goals addressed: Emotional Expressiveness, Improvisational Skills, Listening Skills, Nonverbal Expressiveness, and Verbal Expressiveness.

Space requirements: Enough space for pairs of students to practice offering and accepting offers.

Teacher participation: Coach.

If students are not very emotionally expressive verbally or bodily, this game can help them improve. It requires actors to accept and then "over accept" an offer.

Students create pairs. They decide who will be Actor A, who makes the offer, and Actor B, who over accepts the offer. If Actor A's offer is "That puppy is so cute!" Actor B will first repeat the line in a regular manner to make sure it was heard correctly, then B will *exaggerate* the line verbally and physically as large as possible and explore how large it can be extended. For instance, "That puppy is so cute! That puppy is SOOOOO CUTE! That is the cutest puppy I have EVER SEEN! I can't take my EYES off that PUPPY!" Then switch so Actor A can practice over accepting an offer from Actor B.

This game can be played with all partners working simultaneously, although it will become very LOUD in your classroom. If loud noise would bother other classrooms, play this one pair at a time.

Practicing Improvisation

Knowing how to improvise opens up options to explore all aspects of social-emotional learning. Many school systems required teaching social-emotional skills, also called emotional intelligence or bullying prevention. Teachers have often been handed packets with passive lessons for students to do at their desks, or they have been told to do role play without being given any instruction how to do it.

Social-emotional skills can only be learned through interactive, embodied practice in which students can role play real life situations and practice making choices for themselves. No amount of reading or talking about what to do in an emergency will provide a person with the experience and muscle memory of how to respond. No amount of memorizing the steps of how to negotiate a fair deal or de-escalate a situation will teach students the words for a unique interaction. Practice is what is needed to (a) understand what to do, (b) understand how to do it, (c) find the words necessary at a moment's notice (i.e., improvise), and (d) understand what it feels like to be in a difficult position, while not being intimidated, frightened away, or silenced.

Improvising Life Skills

Many life skills are best taught by acting them out instead of through hearing lectures, watching videos, or reading about them. Improvising situations allow the sequencing of actions, the thought processes, and the feelings that are experienced during a real situation. Scenes can be tailored to the personalities, interests, and abilities of the actors. Keeping scenes unscripted allows unexpected aspects to occur in situations as they do in real life. This is especially useful for helping students learn how to think on their feet.

Here are some simple social situations providing students with practice for real life situations using their improvisational skills. Once a situation has been acted out from beginning to end, students will be ready to put those skills to use in more difficult situations. Choose situations that represent skillsets your students need to work on. For example, students in early primary grades may need to practice introduction skills or how to place a food order on the phone. Older students may need to practice interviewing for a job or asking for appropriate accommodations. Each situation listed below offers an initial set of details in a sequence, but feel free to adapt these as needed.

Introductions

Goals addressed: Eye Contact, Improvisational Skills, Initiation, Introducing Friends to each Other, Introducing Oneself to a New Person, Sequencing, Social Connection, and Social Skills.

Space requirements: This could be done at students' desks or with students at the front of the room. It could also be done in the actor/audience configuration.

Teacher participation: Coach.

Part One – Introducing Two Strangers: Three students volunteer to practice introductions. They can take turns being the friend who knows both people, and the people who will be introduced to each other. Before beginning the scene, talk through what needs to be done by each actor and the order the actions normally happen in. Let the actors practice their parts and practice again after switching parts.

Part Two – Introducing yourself: Two students volunteer to practice meeting each other for the first time. A good situation might include a student who is new to a group (classroom, boy scouts, girl scouts, an after-school club, etc.) and a student who has been there longer. The older member of the group takes the initiative to introducehim/herself and make the new student feel comfortable and welcome. Before doing the first scene, talk through what strangers it would be appropriate to introduce yourself to (e.g., not a stranger on the street!), how to approach the new person in a non-threatening way, how to introduce oneself and ask the new person's name, and how to end with something to make the new person feel comfortable and welcome to the group.

This same situation could be practiced with the new person taking the initiative to introduce him/herself to someone who has been a member of the group.

Then, the second or third situation could be put together with the first situation: One person introduces him/herself to a new person and then takes the new person over to introduce to an old friend. Now the new person knows two people!

Making A Phone Call To A Friend To Plan An Outing

Goals addressed: Asking for permission, Improvisation Skills, Initiation, Listening Skills, Problem-solving, Sequencing, Social Skills, Task Planning and Organization, Verbal Communication, and Working Memory.

Space requirements: Acting area/Audience area.

Teacher participation: Coach.

Supplies required: Two play telephones.

Young children's parents typically arrange playdates for them, but at some point children can begin to take the initiative to plan outings for themselves (with parental permission, of course). This calls for the beginning of planning for oneself, but also sequencing what questions and actions that need to be taken first, second, and third.

This type of scene would need four actors: Two friends and two parents (one for each friend). Have the actors set the stage to create two separate living spaces for the families. Discuss with actors and audience what needs to happen in this situation:

1. Get permission from your parent to ask a friend over to play (or for dinner or to go to the movies, etc.) for a specific day and time.

2. Find the friend's phone number. (Is there a contact sheet from class? Do you already have their phone number on your phone or your mother's phone?)

3. Dial the phone number.

4. If the friend is not old enough for their own phone, the number is probably for a parent's phone. Ask the parent if the friend is at home. (The parent would probably ask who was calling. If the parent did not recognize the name, the parent might ask where they knew their child.)

5. Greet your friend and say who you are.

6. Ask your friend if he/she would like to come over to play on the specific day and time.

7. If the friend says yes, but does not ask their parent first, suggest to your friend to ask for permission.

8. Parent permission is acted out. This means the child must remember the information about the event! The parent might have a few questions if it is not clear what is going to be happening, as well as when and where it will happen.

9. After permission is given, talk about how the two of you are going to get together. Will your family pick the friend up on the way to the movies? Will the friend's parent bring him/her over to your house?)

10. How will the friend get home after the event?

Different options or obstacles could be added for students to practice, such as what do you say if your friend's parent says no, or what if your friend says that day and time is not OK because their family has something else planned, and offers another option.

Ordering Fast Food Delivery

Goals addressed: Asking Permission, Asking for Food Prices and Specials, Creating Consensus, Decision-making, Improvisation Skills, Initiation, Listening Skills, Math Skills, Placing an Order, Sequencing, Social Skills, Task Organization and Planning, Verbal Communication, and Working Memory.

Space requirements: Acting/Audience area.

Teacher participation: Coach.

Supplies needed: Paper, pencil, list of prices for fast food items, and two play telephones.

This kind of scene could include a number of different characters: Student who will be ordering, Restaurant order taker, and Family members who want to place orders.

Discuss what information would be needed in order to place a fast food delivery. What is the order of actions that would need to be taken?

1. What kind of food is going to be ordered? From what restaurant?

2. What is the phone number of the restaurant?

3. What are the prices of the food they sell and are there any specials?

4. What does everyone in the family want to order?

5. What is the delivery address?

6. What will the total price be?

Discuss the order in which actions will need to be taken:

1. Come to consensus with family about what food to order and which restaurant to order from.

2. Call restaurant to get prices and specials. Thank the restaurant person for their help.

3. Go back to family and get their orders.

4. Call back restaurant to place order, give them the delivery address, and get total prices.

Going to a Restaurant

Goals addressed: Behavior Regulation, Decision-making, Emotional Regulation, Improvisation Skills, Initiation, Listening Skills, Sequencing, Social Skills, and Verbal Communication.

Space Requirements: Acting/Audience Area

Teacher participation: Coach.

Supplies needed: Order pad and pencil, menus, plates, cups, and maybe a tray to carry dishes on.

Decide who is going to the restaurant, what meal is going to be eaten, and what kind of restaurant it is. Is a family going for lunch or dinner? Is it a group of friends going for a snack after school? Is it a fancy restaurant, a diner, a family restaurant? Will orders be taken by a waiter or waitress at the table, or will the diners order at a window? What kinds of conversation are appropriate when eating out in public? What other behaviors are appropriate?

Ask for volunteers for the different roles and play out a scenario.

Job Interviews

Goals addressed: Behavior Regulation, Decision-making, Emotional Regulation, Improvisation Skills, Initiation, Listening Skills, Nonverbal Communication, and Verbal Communication.

Space requirements: Acting/Audience area

Teacher participation: Coach.

Supplies needed: "Resume," list of interview questions, list of questions to ask interviewer.

Decide with the group if this interview will be for an after-school job or a summer job. What kind of job? Who will interview potential hires? What kinds of questions would an interviewer ask? Some questions may relate to skills needed for the job, and some may relate to skills needed to relate to customers and co-workers. Sometimes interviewers provide interviewees with potential situations and ask how they would handle it. Usually an interview may end with giving the interviewee a chance to ask questions. What kind of questions are appropriate or inappropriate to ask?

Talk about how to dress for an interview, how to sit while doing an interview (posture, eye contact, etc.), practice handshakes, etc.

Have students interview for different types of jobs. What questions need to be different for these jobs? What questions would probably be the same? Which jobs would the job seeker turn down? Why?

Have a number of students interview for the same job and ask the observers which one they think would have received the job based on the interviews. Which jobs would the job seeker turn down? Why?

Pretend that everyone has interviewed for one of the jobs and have them write a thank you note for the interview they had.

Self-Advocacy: Explaining Accommodations Needed For School Or A Job

Goals addressed: Behavior Regulation, Decision-making, Emotional Regulation, Initiation, Listening Skills, Nonverbal Communication, Prioritizing Skills, Problem-solving, Self-Awareness, and Verbal Communication.

Space requirements: This could be done at students' desks.

Teacher participation: Coach.

Supplies needed: Paper for each student to make a list of accommodations they might need.

It is important for all of us to know how we learn best and if there are accommodations we need to help us learn better or do a better job. Even if we don't have a disability, it is important to receive information in the manner that makes the most sense to us. For instance, I am a good listener, but I am not a great auditory processer in terms of holding onto details about how to do something. I do better if I am given written instructions or if I can take notes on verbal instructions.

It can be hard sometimes to ask for help or to ask for a change in how information is presented. The best way to go about this is in a low key, clear way at the beginning of working with someone, rather than in a stressed or upset manner after a mistake or miscommunication has been made. If it makes sense to relate self-advocacy and accommodation requests to a new job, set up your role playing situation that way. If it makes sense to relate a request to entering a new classroom or joining a new social group, set up your role play that way.

If students are aware of situations in which they do better with specific accommodations, have them verbalize out loud what they need first and then put their needs into words on paper. Coach them to rewrite the request until it is simply worded and explains the needs in a positive, strengths-based manner, explaining how the change will help the person participate/learn/work better. There is no need to apologize for needing an accommodation.

As an example, if someone could not concentrate when an office is filled with a lot of loud conversation and/or music, an accommodation request might read:

> I sometimes have difficulty concentrating if there is a lot of noise from people talking or if there is music playing around me in the office. Whenever there is a noise, I will need to wear headphones to mute the noise. If someone needs to ask me a question, I will be able to hear them and respond, because the headphones don't totally block out noise. They just filter it. I will get more work done, if I can do this.

Once the self-advocacy requests are done, students can practice saying it to another student one-to-one in a warm, open, calm manner, while making eye contact. Students don't need to memorize the request, but they must know their accommodation needs well enough that they can genuinely talk about what they need and why. If students tend to become anxious when asking for an accommodation, encourage them to ground themselves or take some deep breaths before beginning their request. Have the person they are talking to ask a few questions, so the requester has practice flexibly explaining why they need this accommodation.

Conflict Resolution

Conflict-Cooperation Drawings

Goals addressed: Attention, Behavior Regulation, Cognitive Flexibility, Emotional Regulation, Exploring Conflict and Cooperation, Nonverbal Communication, Teamwork, and Turn-taking.

Space requirements: This could be done at students' desks.

Teacher participation: Coach.

Number of players: In pairs.

Supplies required: Two blank pieces of paper for each pair, two different colors of marker for each pair.

This exercise is a great way to begin looking at the differences between conflict and cooperation. Divide students into pairs. Put a blank piece of paper between them on the desk/table. Let each student choose a different color of marker to draw with.

Directions:

> Together you are going to try to make a drawing. It could be a realistic drawing or it could be just a design. Each of you will take turns drawing one line. No speaking between you so you cannot plan what you are doing. For this drawing, you are *not* going to work together. In fact, you may end up trying to stop your partner from accomplishing his/her goals. But you can only do this one line at a time.

Give students between three and five minutes to work. What usually results is a lot of scribbling on the paper as one student tries to cross out the work the other has tried to create. It is also possible that there might end up being two separate designs on the paper – instead of destroying each other's work, they may just ignore each other and work on their own in isolation.

Discuss what happened when they did not work together on their drawing: How did you feel? What does it look like? Is this a useful way to work on a project together? Let students show what happened on their paper.

Then give each pair a new blank piece of paper.

This time each student will work on creating a picture or design, but they will work *together* and try to enhance each other's drawing. No planning ahead of time, and no speaking during the exercise – just pay attention and try to help each other. Again, each one can draw only one line at a time and then the partner gets to draw one line.

Give students five or ten minutes (depending on how focused they are on their work). If some pairs get done and others are engrossed in making an elaborate design, give a three minute warning to come to a stopping point. Tell pairs that are not done that they can finish their drawing later, if they want.

Discuss what happened when they worked together. How did it feel? What were they able to create? Were they able to let go of ideas if their partner added a line they did not expect? Were they able to follow the follower? What is the difference between this drawing and the first one they did? What does this tell you about conflict? What does this tell you about cooperation?

Variation: Group Drawing

Goals addressed: Attention, Behavior Regulation, Cognitive Flexibility, Emotional Regulation, Improvisation Skills, Initiation, Nonverbal Communication, Teamwork, and Turn-taking.

Space requirements: Group of students around a table.

Teacher participation: Coach.

Number of players: Three to five per group.

Supplies needed: A large sheet of paper for each group. Different color markers for each student.

If students enjoyed cooperative drawing, assign an image (a house, a school, a field, a city, a park, etc.) or a design (use only straight lines, only curvy lines, only diamond shapes and squares, etc.) that each group could draw together. Again, students should do this without planning ahead of time and without speaking. They need to pay attention to each other and focus on how they can help create the drawing as a team. Give the group five to ten minutes (depending on age, speed of work, and interest in drawing) for the creation of the drawing.

Share drawings and discuss how each group nonverbally developed a process of working together. Was their group process successful in completing the assignment? Was their group process successful in developing a supportive and interactive team? If the group could make any changes in how they worked together, what would they be?

Helpful Hint: If a group wants to start over, tell them to work with whatever lines were drawn on their paper. Try to incorporate the "mistakes" into the design. If you allow groups to start over

1. instead of drawing improvisationally, they will start becoming perfectionistic and
2. part of the skill set of improvisation is accepting and incorporating mistakes.

Helpful Hint: Remind students that they can "Yes, and …" in drawing as well as in acting.

Helpful Hint: If your class enjoys this kind of drawing, they can improve their group skills even more by mixing into different groups and drawing other pictures or designs. Each time their group process may be different, and they may discover new ways of working together with individuals who have different kinds of skills or different kinds of personalities.

Sculpting Conflict I: Conflict And Resolution

Goals addressed: Behavior Regulation, Body Awareness, Cognitive Empathy, Critical Thinking, Decision-making, Emotional Expression, Emotional Identification, Emotional Intensity Identification, Emotional Regulation, Generating Alternatives, Exploring Conflict and Conflict Resolution, Nonverbal Communication, Problem-solving, Teamwork, and Turn-taking.

Space requirements: A large area of open space.

Teacher participation: Coach.

Number of players: Divide students into groups of four. If there is an uneven number, there could have a group of three or five.

Have each group choose a Sculptor to direct the rest of the group in creating a group picture. Everyone in the group will have a chance to be a Sculptor, so the group may want to go ahead and choose what order they will sculpt in.

The Sculptor decides on a moment of conflict and describes/demonstrates for the others in the group how to embody each sculpted pose.

Be sure the Sculptor knows he/she needs to function as a democratic leader rather than an autocratic or bossy one. The other members of the group are allowed to make suggestions, and the Sculptor, as a good democratic leader, can listen to suggestions and decide to use them or not. However, as the leader, the Sculptor gets the final decision.

Once all the Sculptors are finished, ask students in the sculpts to remember their position and their stance in relationship to each other. Pick a group to begin looking at. All the other groups can relax and gather around the first group. Ask students to look at the group picture and describe what they see. At first try to get them to be very *objective* in their descriptions. No guesses about what might be happening in the scene or what characters might be feeling. For instance:

> I see two people facing each other, looking eye to eye. I see their hands balled up into fists. I see one person standing directly behind the person on the right, leaning out far enough that they can see what the other person is doing.

After the group has objectively described the sculpt, ask them to *subjectively* describe it. In other words, can they intuit what kind of characters these are and their relationships or the kind of situation it is. For instance, for the picture described above:

> I think maybe these two are about to get into a fight, and it looks like either the person behind the fighter on the right is egging him on. Or maybe the fighter on the left did something bad to the one standing behind, and the fighter on the right is protecting him.

After all the objective and subjective descriptions are made, ask the sculptor what he/she had in mind when setting up the sculpt. Then move onto the next group sculpt.

After all the group sculpts have been looked at and described, ask the Sculptor to make a second sculpt that resolves the conflict in some way. It doesn't have to necessarily be a peaceful resolution. Once these are done, remind the actors being statues to remember their positions and relax. Move around to each of the groups in the same order as before and ask the class how the conflict was resolved – first, *objectively*, then *subjectively*.

Allow another member of the group to be a sculptor and begin the process again.

Sculpting Conflict II: Conflict And Resolution

Goals addressed: Behavior Regulation, Body Awareness, Cognitive Empathy, Critical Thinking, Decision-making, Emotional Expression, Emotional Identification, Emotional Intensity Identification, Emotional Regulation, Generating Alternatives, Exploring Conflict and Conflict Resolution, Improvisation Skills, Nonverbal Communication, Problem-solving, Teamwork, and Turn-taking.

Space requirements: A large area of open space.

Teacher participation: Coach.

Number of players: Divide students into groups of four. If there is an uneven number there, could be a group of three or five.

This exploration begins the same way the last one did. Everyone in the group will have a chance to create a group sculpt, so have the group choose what order they want to be Sculptor.

The Sculptor decides on a moment of conflict and describes/demonstrates for the others in the group how to embody those people in a sculpted pose.

Once all the Sculptors are finished, ask each student in the sculpts to remember their position and their stance in relationship to the others. Pick a group to begin looking at. All the other groups can relax and gather around the first group. Ask students to look at the statue and describe what they see. At first try to get them to be very *objective* in their descriptions. No guesses about what might be happening in the scene or what characters might be feeling.

After the group has objectively described the sculpt, then ask them to *subjectively* describe it. In other words, can they intuit what kind of characters these are, their relationships or the situation.

After the objective and subjective descriptions are expressed, ask the sculptor what he/she had in mind when setting up the sculpt. Then move onto the next group sculpt.

When the group sculpts have been looked at and described, ask the sculptor to create a story with a beginning, middle, and end. The current sculpt is the height of the conflict. Through a scene, show how the conflict started and how it got to this point. Then show how the conflict is resolved.

If one of the suggestions by the class is more interesting to the Sculptor than what he/she originally had in mind, the Sculptor can opt to create a scene using that situation and characters.

Helpful Hint: If a scene depicts a fight of some kind, ask students to enact the violence through slow motion. This will keep them in control of their bodies, and no one will get hurt. In addition, make sure no violent gesture by one actor actually touches another. Explain to students that in the movies and TV what looks like violence is really called "stage combat" and is very safe and nonviolent. Movie and TV actors' fight scenes are actually more like dances that have been carefully choreographed and practiced for hours so no one is ever hurt. Students often have a lot of fun creating slow-motion conflicts.

When the groups are ready, allow each to show their scene.

Discuss how the characters resolved the situation. If the group chose to resolve the scene in a negative way (i.e., through violence), ask that group to see if they could find a way to resolve the conflict without violence. If the group resolved the conflict unrealistically or "magically," ask them to see if they could find a way to resolve it more realistically, through their own give and take. If the group resolved their scene in a positive, non-violent way, ask them to see if they can find *another* positive, nonviolent solution to the conflict. Give groups time to decide how to change their scenes, then share with the whole group.

Allow another member of the group to be a sculptor for their group and begin the process again.

Helpful Hint: These sculpting exercises are usually enjoyed by students and get them thinking about options for dealing with difficult situations. The more they enjoy creating them, the longer it often takes to get through a round of scenes. I believe it is important for each person to have a chance to be a sculptor if they want to. It is important for self-efficacy for students to take the responsibility of democratically directing the other members of their group without dictating to them or ordering them around. It is possible to work on a round of scenes, then continue with another round in another drama session. If you do this, make sure to keep the groups the same so that everyone has a chance to be the Sculptor. If, because of personality conflicts, it becomes necessary to switch someone out of a group, be sure to switch with another person who has had the same sculpting opportunity (either both had sculpted or both had not).

Scenes Of Escalation And De-Escalation

Goals addressed: Behavior Regulation, Cognitive Flexibility, Decision-making, Emotional Regulation, Exploring Conflict and Conflict Resolution,

Improvisation Skills, Inhibition, Initiation, Listening Skills, Problem-solving, Shifting Emotions, Stress Management, Teamwork, and Verbal Communication.

Space requirements: Acting/Audience Space.

Teacher participation: Coach.

Go over the information about how a conflict can be escalated or de-escalated that are on the pages that follow this exercise. Create short fictional situations for each of the escalation techniques and its opposite de-escalation technique. This will help students clearly differentiate them and understand how they work.

Helpful Hint: As students act out situations, they may find themselves actually being physically and emotionally escalated and de-escalated. Be prepared to catch a scene before escalation goes over the top and gets out of control. If an actor starts to be overtaken by the emotions of the char-acter being played, call a freeze to the scene and ask for the other actor to start de-escalating the scene. In the best of all possible worlds, the best intervention is to move to de-escalation techniques before this happens. However, when that does not happen, be prepared to step in and side coach.

Helpful Hint: Be prepared to side coach the scene with suggestions for escalation and de-escalation as shown in Table 4.1, if students get stuck or are worried about "looking mean." Remind them that they are playing a fictional character and helping the class learn about conflict and conflict resolution.

Helpful Hint: If an actor gets upset during a scene of conflict because the emotions of the character are so strong, freeze the scene. Check to see if the actor is truly upset or just doing a really good job of acting. If the actor really is upset, guide him/her to breathe deeply and slowly to calm down. Remind the actor that this is a fictional scene, and sometimes when begin-ning actors are playing fictional characters, they actually start to feel the feelings of their character. That is normal, but you want them to remain in control of themselves as an actor. Grounding and staying calm deep inside will allow an actor to express an emotion without being overwhelmed by their feelings. You can also give the actor(s) who got upset the opportunity to have someone take over the role for them if they need time to decom-press. I do not expect that this situation will happen often, but I always want teachers and counselors to have an idea of how to handle an unusual situation when it occurs.

Table 4.1

WAYS TO ESCALATE VIOLENCE	WAYS TO DE-ESCALATE VIOLENCE
Stop listening. "I've heard enough." "You don't know what you are doing!"	**Listen.** "Tell me more." Ask for more details.
Interrupt or cross talk.	**Allow the other person to finish what he is saying before responding.**
Listen to only parts of what is said: It's easy to misunderstand if you've only heard part.	**Listen reflectively and check out meaning** "I am hearing you say this_____. Did I get that right?"
Deny others' feelings and their right to have those feelings.	**Validate the feelings others express.** "I would feel angry if that happened, too."
React strongly and negatively.	**Wait until you hear more until you react.**
Assume the other side has nothing of value to contribute to the community or to solving the problem.	**Assume the other side has wisdom, ideas, and potential solutions you haven't thought of yet.**
Only think about YOUR needs or wants: "It's my way or no way!" "You don't count."	**Remember that others will have different points of view, needs, and wants. Try to consider both theirs and yours.**
Use words to hurt or intimate.	**Use words to heal and encourage.**
Disrespect and insult the other side: Name calling! Put downs!	**Show respect/be polite.** Empathize with the other person.
Oppress the other/give them no say.	**Empower the other/share power.**
Control all the options. Offer only one choice.	**Include others in the planning.** **Brainstorm solutions openly.**
Try to seize power.	**Negotiate/offer to share power.**
Isolate/keep to yourself or your group.	**Team with others/work together.**
Share no personal information.	**Open up/be generous.**
Use a Win/Lose Strategy (So, you will win and they will lose!)	**Use a Win/Win Strategy: Look for ways for everyone to get what they want and need.**
Bring in past history or other topics.	**Keep to the topic of discussion.**
Blame the other person "You make me feel _____"	**Take responsibility for your own feelings, thoughts, and actions.**

WAYS TO ESCALATE VIOLENCE	WAYS TO DE-ESCALATE VIOLENCE
Think in terms of "Us and Them."	Think in terms of "we" or "community."
Use words like ALWAYS & NEVER	Use words like "sometimes" or "this time"
Define things in terms of "life and death" "evil and good."	Realize that life is more often a continuum instead of either/or.
Be as nasty as you can so the other side will know how strongly you feel.	Use kindness and positive statements.
Act without thinking.	Think about the consequences of your actions before you take them!
Use words and actions to threaten or hurt.	Use actions to solve problems and create trust and goodwill

Always de-role after acting out scenes of escalations and de-escalations!

Observing Escalation/De-Escalation On Video

Goals addressed: Behavior Regulation, Cognitive Empathy, Emotional Identification, Exploring Conflict and Conflict Resolution, Listening Skills, Observation Skills, and Shifting Emotions.

Space requirements: This could be done at students' desks.

Teacher participation: Coach.

Supplies required: Video clips of scenes of conflict.

Find video clips of scenes of conflict to show conflict being escalated and/or de-escalated. Have students watch and identify which skills (for good or for ill) are being used in the scene. They may need to watch the scene more than once to pick out all the examples. Then discuss the scene as a class.

Good examples (depending on age) of appropriate scenes of conflict can be found in: *Sandlot, The Princess Bride, Willow, The War, West Side Story,* and if your students are older, in many scenes from Shakespeare. Particularly good scenes of conflict can be found in *Romeo and Juliet, A Midsummer Night's Dream,* and *The Tempest.* There are many videos of Shakespeare's plays online and on digital video disc (DVD).

Emotion Targets

Goals addressed: Behavioral Regulation, Emotional Expression, Emotional Regulation, Recognizing Emotional Triggers, Shifting Emotions, and Stress Management.

Space requirements: Desks or tables will be needed for artwork. Later, an area big enough for pinning or taping up targets and standing back to throw something at them. This will depend on the throwing abilities of the students.

Teacher participation: Coach.

Supplies needed: Paper plates, colored markers, wet tissues or bean bags to throw, tape or thumbtacks to put targets up with.

Each participant creates a drawing with colored markers that is a visual metaphor of a feeling or problem that is upsetting them on a paper plate. The plate is taped or pinned to the wall. The participants throw bean bags or wet tissues at the target and as they throw, they can make a noise that expresses letting go of their anger or frustration.

Helpful Hint: Using wet tissues creates a lovely thump and smears the image in a way that can be very satisfying.

Always De-role Afterwards!

Dealing with Peer Pressure

Sometimes it is difficult to resist peer pressure, even when peers want you to join in with something you know you should not be doing. This is as true for adults as it is for children. There is a reason for this: Human beings are social animals and want to belong. Connecting with others is one of the ways our species survived over the millennia. Whenever there is strong motivation to follow what appears to be approved by a majority of peers, there is also a strong fear of being rejected by them if they are not followed.

Standing up to peer pressure takes a lot of courage and belief in one's own values and ideas. This requires understanding what those values are. Before enacting scenes about resisting peer pressure, it may be helpful to have a discussion about what the values underlying the conflict are. Then students will be acting out something they have thought through and committed to take a stand for, instead of "Just saying no."

Telling The Truth When Under Pressure To Lie

Goals addressed: Behavior Regulation, Cognitive Empathy, Critical Thinking, Decision-making, Emotional Regulation, Generating Alternatives, Improvisation Skills, Problem-solving, Self-Reflection, Social Skills, and Verbal Communication.

Space requirements: Acting/Audience areas.

Teacher participation: Coach.

Discuss why it is important to tell the truth. Then ask questions related to dishonesty. What are reasons lying could hurt someone else? What are consequences that could happen to you if later it was discovered that you had lied? What feelings come up when someone is about to lie? What about after someone has lied?

With the class, brainstorm situations in which someone could be pressured to lie for another person or to lie for oneself. Choose several situations to act out.

After each scene, ask the actors what their character felt when they lied or when they were lied to? What do they think might happen in the future to their characters because of the lie? Be sure to de-role the actors after the scene.

If useful, replay the scene and have the character who lied tell the truth. Discuss what was different this time (besides just telling the truth). It is possible the truth got someone else or that character in trouble? What are the results of that pro and con?

Saying "No, thanks" to Thrill-Seeking Behavior

Goals addressed: Assertiveness, Behavior Regulation, Cognitive Empathy, Critical Thinking, Decision-making, Emotional Regulation, Generating Alternatives, Improvisation Skills, Problem-solving, Self-Reflection, Social Skills, and Verbal Communication.

Space requirements: Acting/Audience areas.

Teacher participation: Coach.

Discuss what thrill-seeking behavior is. Sometimes thrill seeking is OK. For instance, rides at an amusement park can be thrilling, as can scary movies. However, some kinds of thrill-seeking behavior like shoplifting or carrying a gun can get the seeker in legal trouble. Other thrill-seeking behavior like drag racing or jumping off a moving truck can get the thrill-seeker injured or kill. Often people are pressured into doing thrill seeking with their friends. Sometimes a whole group gets involved in thrill seeking when most of them would rather not, but they are too afraid to say no because they might appear to be scared or "nerdy" or "goody-goody."

Brainstorm situations that people your students' age might feel pressured to engage in by their friends. Pick a few scenes to act out. In the scene, practice ways of saying no to the group before they undertake their thrill-seeking adventure. Practice ways of saying no after you have already gone with the group. It's never too late to back out of a bad idea!

Derole after each scene and discuss feelings and potential consequences that were involved.

Saying "No, Thanks" To Using Drugs, Alcohol, Tobacco, And E-Cigarettes

Using drugs, alcohol, tobacco, and e-cigarettes are types of thrill-seeking behaviors attached to peer pressure. These substances have a very specific negative consequence: Addiction and other types of health problems. There are so many ways addiction can ruin a life. Unfortunately, many media examples of addiction, fictional and nonfictional, make it appear glamorous. Approaching saying no to drugs by using any kind of exaggeration or scare tactics usually backfires, because students become curious to find out more and experience what it feels like. Even statistics or reports about how many people have died from certain types of substances fall flat because children and teens typically are in denial that they are ever going to die.

Unglamorous examples of the results of addiction, like the cigarette commercials by the Truth Initiative (www.truthinitiative.org) that have been running the past several years on television, seem to have been effective. The testimonials are not by actors, but by people who have visually been negatively affected by smoking. Because of the work of the Truth Initiative along with other anti-smoking campaigns, youth smoking has decreased from 23% in 2000 to 3% in 2020 (https://truthinitiative.org/who-we-are/our-impact). Unfortunately, many young people substituted vaping for smoking because it was promoted as a healthy substitute. By 2019 one million youth vaped every day and 1.6 million vaped at least 20 times a month (https://www.singlecare.com/blog/news/vaping-statistics/).

In 2018, the Truth Initiative began a campaign against opioids (https://www.thetruth.com/o/opioids). Videos that depict drug addiction as it really is are usually filled with images and language that are not appropriate for high school students, let alone for those in elementary school.

The Drug Abuse Resistance Education (D.A.R.E) Program which ran in 75 percent of U.S. public schools from 1983 to 2009 was found by over 30 research studies to not work at stopping students from experimenting with drugs and alcohol (Nordrum, 2014). This was because it was based on scare tactics and lecturing at children. A new program was developed by psychologists and implemented in 2013 focused on decision-making for a healthy life (Nordrum, 2014). However, it appears from subsequent research studies of the *new* program that this one is no better, even though it has been given approval by Substance Abuse and Mental Health Services Administration National Registry of Evidence-based Programs and Practices (SAMSHA NREPP) (Caputi & McLellan, 2016; Ingraham, 2017).

Needless to say, trying to encourage students to say "No, thanks" to addictive substances is difficult to achieve in school. The same can be said for bullying programs (which will be addressed in the next section). Does this mean that drug education should be avoided because it is a waste of time? I tend to think that *any* kind of decision-making or assertiveness roleplaying will help encourage students' problem-solving skills and behavioral regulation. If you are using this book on a regular basis with your students, most likely you are providing them with at least a partial inoculation against drugs as they become better able to inhibit rash behavior choices, learn how to organize and plan their thoughts and behaviors, and become more self-reflective and discerning,

In my experience as a drama therapist working with adult recovering substance abusers, I have found that almost every one of them experienced childhood abuse, neglect, and trauma. Out of over one thousand clients I worked with, only one ever said to me, "I got started on drugs because of peer pressure." No one ever told me it was because they took a dare to try something and then got "hooked."

Most addicts have a genetic vulnerability to become addicted. They seek out addictive substances to help numb out the pain they are carrying around from trauma they experienced. They fall in love with the feelings of euphoria the substance gives them … for a while. Then their brain structure and chemistry changes, and they require more and more drugs to create the same effect. A genetic vulnerability to addiction is not going to be fixed through drama. Trauma can be worked on through drama therapy, but that is not part of the skill set or job description of a classroom teacher and rarely even that of a school counselor.

If you want to address the dangers of driving while under the influence of a mind-altering substance or riding in a car with a driver who is under the influence, that kind of scene may be useful for teens, just as a scene about not texting while driving would be useful. If students request to act out scenes in which they say no to a cigarette, e-cigarette, beer, pills, or opioids, follow their lead. Obviously they have some questions that they want to explore. There is nothing ever wrong with practicing assertiveness.

Bullying

United Nations Educational Scientific and Cultural Organization (UNESCO) acknowledges that bullying is a universal problem. They define bullying this way:

> A learner is bullied when s/he is exposed repeatedly over time to aggressive behaviour that intentionally inflicts injury or discomfort through physical contact, verbal attacks, fighting or psychological manipulation. Bullying involves an imbalance of power and can include teasing, taunting, use of hurtful nicknames, physical violence or social exclusion. A bully can operate alone or within a group of peers. Bullying may be direct, such as one child demanding money or possessions from another, or indirect, such as a group of students spreading rumours about another. Cyber bullying is harassment through e-mail, cell phones, text messages and defamatory websites. (2009, p.11)

UNESCO reports that 32% of all school children have been bullied at least once in the last month (2019). That percentage is equal for girls and boys. In the United States, psychological bullying, including cyber bullying, is more common than physical bullying (UNESCO, 2019). Data shows that bullying is higher in upper elementary school grades (43% at ages nine and ten) than at older ages (33% at ages 13–14 and 32% at age 15), however, the type of bullying changes as students get older. Physical bullying decreases, and cyber bullying increases (UNESCO, 2019). Between 2002 and 2014 the overall rate of bullying has had a small decrease in the US, but cyber bulling has increased as computer use has grown.

Physical difference is the biggest reason for bullying at 15.3% (disability, obesity, etc.) then race, nationality, or color (10.9%), followed by religion (4.6%) (UNESCO, 2019). Bullying affects students' grades, attendance at school, and mental health. Students become anxious, depressed, and often cannot sleep at night, because they are worrying about going back to school the next day. In UNESCO's 2019 report *Behind the Numbers: Ending School Violence and Bullying,* 23% of bullied children contemplated suicide and 30% became involved in the abuse of alcohol, 20% started smoking tobacco, and 8% began smoking marijuana (UNESCO, 2019). Here is where the danger of addiction to drugs and alcohol can be found, and it is in response to on-going daily trauma, not peer pressure.

Negotiation author and expert William Ury, in his book *Getting to Peace* (1999), explains that there are three sides to any conflict, not two. In the case of bullying, the three sides are the bully, the victim, and the community. The community has a vested interest in resolving the conflict, because bullying disrupts cooperation and peace. Part of the community are the bystanders to bullying incidents. Mostly bystanders are passive witnesses, because they do not know what to do to intervene. Without appropriate skills, they fear they won't know what to say, could be pulled into the conflict, and possibly become victims, too.

In case you believe that bullying is a normal rite of passage that children and teens need to experience as part of growing up, think again. Research reveals that children who have been bullied have more symptoms of depression, anxiety, and other psychiatric disorders than children who have not. These disorders continue into adulthood. Victims of bullies are 4.3 times more likely to have an anxiety disorder as an adult. Bullies who were also victims are 14.5 times more likely to develop panic disorder, 4.8 times more likely to be diagnosed with depression, and 18.5 times more likely to have suicidal thoughts as adults (Saint Louis, 2013).

The most successful interventions in lowering bullying have been bystander intervention programs, followed by the creation of a positive school climate with peer conciliation and mediation, teachers and administrators who are not afraid to intervene, and counseling for bullies and victims (UNESCO, 2019). It would appear that providing bystander intervention practice may be the most effective way to help practice assertiveness skills and "inoculate" students against becoming victims or bully victims. (Bully victim is the term for students who after being bullied project their anger, frustration, and feelings of helplessness onto other classmates who serve as their victim.)

Sculpts And Scenes Involved In A Bullying Situation

Goals addressed: Assertiveness, Behavior Regulation, Cognitive Empathy, Critical Thinking, Emotional Expression, Emotional Regulation, Improvisational Skills, Initiation, Nonverbal Communication, Self-Reflection, and Verbal Communication.

Space requirements: An open space in which students can sculpt each other.

Teacher participation: Coach.

Number of players: Students in groups of four.

Divide your students into groups of four or five and within their group have them pair off to sculpt each other in the four potential roles for a bullying scenario.

The roles involved in a bullying scenario include:

- the bully
- the bully's ally
- the bullied (aka victim)
- the bystander

There is a good chance that everyone in your class has played all of these roles at one time or another. Have the group decide how these roles might relate to each other in a scenario of their choice and ask them to invent a few sentences for each role to say about how they feel and what they want to do at this moment.

After all of the sculpts are done, ask the students to remember their positions and their stance in relationship to the others. Pick a group to begin looking at. All the other groups can relax and gather around the first group. Ask students to identify who in the scene is the bully, the bully's ally, the bullied, and the bystander. What *objective information* reveals who is playing each role? Check with the group being observed and see if the roles were identified correctly. Then ask each actor to share what their character feels and what their character might want to do if the sculpt came alive in this moment.

Discuss what would have to happen for the bystander to change from a passive witness into an assertive ally for the bullied. What are some things they could say or do to help in this specific situation?

When each group has shared their sculpts, give them time to develop and practice their scenario. Then each group can share their work with the rest of the class. After each scene, discuss the choices that were made. Were they realistic? Were they effective? Were they appropriate for the time and place in which the scene took place? Were there different actions that could have been taken for the scene to end successfully for the ally and the bullied?

If there is only time to sculpt and discuss the roles in each group, the actual scenes could be acted out in a different session. If helpful, have students replay the scenes to illustrate different successful and appropriate ways to help.

At the end of acting out any bully scenes, if the person playing the bullied feels as if they would like to talk back to their bully and put him/her in their place, give them the time to say what their character might say.

Always de-role afterwards!

Notes

1. The "straight man" is a comedy term for the person in the team who sets up the jokes for the comedian. That is, the straight man "plays it straight" and acts in a deeply serious manner or an innocent and naïve one. The "straight man" does not have to be "straight" or a "man." Another term for this is "comic foil." Famous "comic foils" include Bud Abbott of "Who's on first?" fame (Abbott and Costello), Vivian Vance, who set up jokes for Lucille Ball (*I Love Lucy*), and Bob Newhart who set up all the rest of the characters in his TV sit coms.

2. When a problem in a scene is not solved by the characters them-selves, but by an unexpected late comer to the scene or a magical intervention that comes out of nowhere, that is called a *deus ex machina* which literally translates as "god in the machine." In Ancient Greek theatre, playwrights who did not know how to end their play would have a "god" descend from "the heavens" to save the protag-onist. The actor was lowered on a machine that was similar to our

mechanical crane. Lazy playwrights who write their characters into a corner sometimes use this technique to bring a play to an end, but it is very unsatisfying for an audience, because the play has not shown how the problem could be solved.

References

Belt, L., & Stockley, R. (1989). *Improvisation through theatre sports*. Thespis Productions.

Caputi, T. L., & McLellan, A. T. (2016). Truth and D.A.R.E.: Is DARE's new keepin' it REAL curriculum suitable for American nationwide implementation? *Drugs: Education, Prevention and Policy, 24*(1), pp. 49–57. Available at: https://doi.org/10.1080/09687637.2016.1208731

Dudeck, T. R., & McClure, C. (Eds.) (2018). *Applied improvisation: Leading, collaborating and creating beyond the theatre*. Methuen.

Ingraham, C. (2017, July 12). A brief history of DARE, the anti-drug program Jeff Sessions wants to revive. *The Washington Post*. Available at: https://www.washingtonpost.com/news/wonk/wp/2017/07/12/a-brief-history-of-d-a-r-e-the-anti-drug-program-jeff-sessions-wants-to-revive/

Johnstone, K. (1981). *Impro: Improvisation and the theatre*. Routledge.

Lanzoni, S. (2018). *Empathy: A history*. Yale University Press.

Leonard, K., & Yorton, T. (2015). *Lessons from the Second City Yes, and: How improvisation reverses "No, but" thinking and improves creativity and collaboration*. HarperCollins.

Nordrum, A. (2014, September 10). The new D.A.R.E. program–This one works. *Scientific American Mind*. Available at: https://www.scientificamerican.com/article/the-new-d-a-r-e-program-this-one-works/

Patinkin, S. (2000). *The second city: Backstage at the world's greatest comedy theater*. Sourcebooks, Inc.

Reiss, H. (2018). *The empathy effect: 7 neuroscience-based keys for transforming the way we live, love, work, and connect across difference*. Sounds True.

Saint Louis, C. (2013, February 20). Effects of bullying last into adulthood, study finds. *NYTimes.com*. Retrieved from http://well.blog.nytimes.com/2013/02/20/effects-of-bullying-last-into-adulthood.

Sternberg, P., & Garcia, A. (2000). *Sociodrama: Who's in Your Shoes?* 2nd ed., Praeger.

The Truth Initiative. Available at: http://www.truthinitiative.org

UNESCO. (2009). *Stopping violence in schools: A guide for teachers.* UNESCO.

UNESCO. (2019). *Behind the numbers: Ending school violence and bullying.* UNESCO.

Ury, W. (1999). *Getting to peace: Transforming conflict at home, at work, and in the world.* Viking.

Wasson, S. (2017). *Improv nation: How we made a great American art.* Houghton Mifflin Harcourt Publishing Company.

Using Drama to Enhance the Learning of Academic Subjects

Introduction

Once you have experience leading drama games and facilitating improvisations, you can begin to include drama in your teaching skill set. As mentioned in Chapter One, embodied experience with academic subjects engage students more deeply and help them remember material better. The guiding assumption in embodied learning is that "cognition is grounded in bodily interactions with the environment and culture, and that abstract concepts are tied to the body's sensory and motor system" (Fugate, Macrine, & Cipriano, 2019, p. 274). When experience is processed though sensory and perceptual systems, the brain is able to pull up the memories of the embodied knowledge later to re-create the experience in the mind, thinking it through by simulating it internally. In essence, the student has created a rich, personal experience, which can then be remembered and used for problem-solving.

A variety of researchers have demonstrated this in classroom experiments. For instance, when students use toys and miniatures to simulate the actions in a story they are reading, their comprehension increases, allowing them to imagine the story more clearly. "First and second graders who underwent this approach recalled 33% more information (compared to those who had toys or objects present, but were not allowed to manipulate them)" (Fugate et al., 2019, p. 280). Writing by hand with a pencil or pen allows for "richer encoding of the information which allows a better representation from which [students] can later draw" than students who use a computer keyboard (Fugate et al.,

2019, p. 281). Both concrete manipulatives and finger counting have been shown to promote better numerical processing in the early years of learning math; later this translates into more ability in advanced subjects like calculus (Fugate et al., 2019). In science, research has shown that hands-on and embodied experiences promote a clearer understanding of concepts in a lesson, compared with students who only watched a demonstration and listened to a lecture about it. Even the use of gestures improve learning both when used by the educator imparting information and by students explaining or discussing their understanding of a subject. This is thought to be true because gestures create physical, moving metaphors that concretely represent the meaning of the information being conveyed (Shapiro & Stolz, 2019). Drama is immersive of the whole child and like embodied science lessons, can make other curricular subjects enticing and concrete.

Keith Sawyer, a psychologist who has studied the use of improvisation in the classroom, advocates for an improvisational and embodied approach to teaching. He feels this is the strongest approach because:

> Each student starts with a different set of knowledge, and each student might take a different path toward creative knowledge. That's why learning is most effective when the teacher improvisationally responds to each student's needs in each moment. (2019, p. 36)

A group leader who understands improvisation's "Yes, and …" builds on the insights their students have and is fearless in inventing new ways to explore those insights, whether they be through creative enactments of physics or bringing a moment of history to life. Putting students into action and allowing them to solve problems, rather than giving them answers to memorize, leads to critical thinking abilities and information that

1. Go into long-term memory and
2. Can be accessed through different recall avenues whenever needed.

This means the leader creates the scaffolding needed to get the students started on their explorations, so they can grasp the big picture as well as the details of it.

> [Whenever students'] knowledge is a complex conceptual system, able to stand on its own … the teacher *fades* the scaffold. "Fading" is a process where the teacher monitors the classroom's progress, and in response, carefully and slowing removes the guiding structures, as students gain more and more understanding. (Sawyer, 2019, p. 60)

What follows are a variety of explorations that could be incorporated into traditional subjects to scaffold students' mastery of material through action.

Language Arts

Alphabet Race (Aycox, 1999)

Goals addressed: Letter recognition, Sequencing, Spelling, and Teamwork.

Space requirements: Enough space for two parallel lines of students and one long table or two smaller tables in front of each line.

Teacher/Counselor participation: Coach.

Supplies needed: Two sets of alphabet cards, 26 letters on cards approximately four inches by four inches or bigger. If possible, each set should be a different color.

The Leader calls out a word to be spelled. (It cannot have any double letters in it, unless each team has at least two sets of cards!) For instance, if the Leader calls out "Pencil," the first six players on each team rush to their table, pick up the letters needed for that word and arrange themselves to spell the word. The first player in line picks up P, the second picks up E, etc. When the team turns around, they must be standing so that the word can be read from left to right. The first team to spell the word correctly earns a point. After the word is spelled, the letters are put back on the table. They do not have to be kept in alphabetical order, unless you wish them to be placed that way.

Helpful Hint: This could be a wonderful review game before a weekly spelling test.

Body-Spelling

Goals addressed: Body Control, Gross Motor Skills, Sequencing, Spelling, and Teamwork.

Space requirements: Open space where students can move.

Teacher/Counselor participation: Leader and Coach.

Preparation: Count the number of letters in each word in the week's vocabulary list and categorize the words with the same number together.

Round One: Players gather in groups with the same number of letters as the word that is going to be spelled. A version of Amoeba can be played to do this: Players wander around the room in a random fashion. The Leader calls out the number of letters in a set of spelling words. Players quickly get into a group of that number. If there is a "remainder" that is not large enough for the number that has been called out, those players can help the Leader judge if the word is spelled correctly. The students who have been part of the "remainder" will need to be included in the next round.

Once players are in the right sized group, the Leader calls out the vocabulary words. The group must spell the word using their bodies to create the shape of the letters in the word: Each player makes one letter in the correct order. The Leader checks to see if the word is correctly spelled. If it is, the class goes onto the next word on the list. If it is not, they need to look at one of the other groups that has spelled the word correctly and adjust their spelling.

When all of the vocabulary words with that number of letters have been spelled out, have the class create "amoebas" again to randomly reform into new groups of a different number and continue spelling out words.

Round Two: The Leader calls out each word on the list, and players spell out all the letters of the word in order with their bodies. To keep everyone together, players say each letter out loud as they make them. If someone says the wrong letter (meaning they are in the process of spelling the word incorrectly), freeze the group so the player can re-configure the letter to be with the rest of the class. A word that many players are struggling with can be spelled more than once to rehearse the correct spelling.

Pressure Nouns (Aycox, 1999)

Goals addressed: Generating Alternatives, Identifying the Parts of Speech, and Working under Pressure.

Space requirements: Students sitting in a circle.

Teacher/Counselor participation: Leader and Coach.

Supplies required: An object that is easy to pass like a Magic Tube or Talking Stick.

One person is It and stands in the center of the circle with the object to be passed. It hands the object to someone in the circle. That person says, "A" and passes the object to the person on the left or the right, who says, "B," and so on around the circle. Whenever It chooses, It will point at a person who has just said a letter. This person must name six nouns (no proper nouns) that begin with that letter. Meanwhile, the object is silently continuing to be passed around the circle. The Namer must complete all six nouns by the time the object comes back. If the Namer does not succeed, he or she becomes It, and It sits down. If the Namer does get all six nouns said, then It continues for the next round.

Helpful Hint: How many nouns get named depends on the size of the group. The larger the group, the more words should be required so the pressure is on.

Variation: You can substitute other parts of speech for noun: Pronoun, verb, adjective, adverb, or even proper noun.

Variation: Use this game to help in the learning of a foreign language. Beginners can name six words that start with the letter in that language. Later, when they know more words, they could name six words of a specific part of speech in the language.

Helpful Hint: This game can be used to help students work under pressure. Lead them in a guided breathing exercise before starting the game and coach them to keep breathing if they begin to get tense. This kind of practice dealing with pressure will help them cope with timed tests.

In the Manner of the Word

Goals addressed: Gross Motor Skills, Identification of Parts of Speech, Improvisational Skills, Non-verbal Communication, Observation Skills, and Turn-taking

Space requirements: Students sitting in a circle or in an Acting/Audience arrangement.

Teacher/Counselor participation: Leader and Coach.

Adverbs are written down on slips of paper and put into one envelop or container while action verbs are written down on slips of paper and put into another. Players take turns picking one slip of paper from each envelop and act out the verb in the manner the adverb. The observing players guess first the verb and then the adverb.

I'm Thinking Of A Word That Rhymes With … (Aycox, 1999)

Goals addressed: Attention, Behavioral Regulation, Generating Alternatives, Gross Motor Skills, Improvisational Skills, Inhibition, Non-verbal Communication, Observation Skills, Recognition of Words that Rhyme, Turn-taking, and Teamwork.

Space requirements: Enough room for two teams to be opposite each other with space in between them for acting.

Teacher/Counselor participation: Leader and Coach.

Supplies required: Pencil and paper for each team.

Each team thinks of four or five target words. Then they think of a word that rhymes with each of the words. Then they decide an order in which the players will take turns. When both sides are ready, the Leader chooses one side to start. The first player on that team steps forward and says, "I'm thinking of a word that rhymes with [and says the word that was chosen to rhyme with the target word]." For example, "I'm thinking of a word that rhymes with cat."

The other team follows their player order. Instead of guessing the rhyming word out loud, the player has to pantomime a word that rhymes with cat. They might pantomime hitting a baseball with a bat. If bat is not the target word, the player on the first side says, "No, it's not bat." The next player on the guessing side gets up and might pantomime putting on a hat. The player on the first team says, "No, it's not hat." This continues until the correct word is pantomimed. If a player on the guessing team has an idea that needs to be acted out with more than one person, the member of the team next to them can help.

After the first team guesses correctly or gives up, the other side takes a turn until all the words have been guessed.

Helpful Hint: The group can decide a limit to the number of guesses that can be made, or the guessing team can continue until they guess the correct answer or give up.

Helpful Hint: Before starting, the Leader should check the words of each team to make sure that they do not have the same rhyme sound in their words because the game can become boring if the same words are constantly being pantomimed.

Helpful Hint: The Leader also needs to make sure that the target word and the word that sounds like it, really do rhyme. Sometimes words look like they should rhyme, but they do not. This doublecheck is particularly important for younger players who are just learning about words that rhyme.

Helpful Hint: Remind players on the team giving the word not to blurt out the correct word or act out the correct word, but to focus on identifying the word being acted out that rhymes with it.

Haiku Activities

Goals addressed: Learning about haiku, Rhythm, Syllable Recognition, Self-Reflection, and Verbal Communication.

Space requirements: Students could be at their desks.

Teacher/Counselor participation: Leader and Coach.

Supplies needed: Paper and pencil, Writing surface.

A Haiku is a Japanese poem that has three lines. The first and last line have five syllables and the middle line has seven syllables. Usually, haiku do not rhyme. Haiku are often written about nature or a special moment and lead the reader to a greater appreciation of a moment in time.

Explain the structure of a haiku and give students five to ten minutes to create one about themselves or about something they like. Read each other the haiku. After sharing, the authors could illustrate their haiku. Perhaps in small groups, authors could create a sculpt or movement that expresses the haiku with their group members.

Secret Agenda

Goals addressed: Cognitive Flexibility, Critical Thinking, Listening Skills, Storytelling, Turn-taking, Verbal Communication, and Vocabulary Enhancement.

Space requirements: Students sitting in a circle or at their desks.

Teacher/Counselor participation: Leader and Coach.

Supplies required: A pencil and one index card per player.

Each player writes an unusual or uncommon word or phrase on their index card. Then the Leader picks one player to begin a story. As the first teller begins the story, they must use their word or phrase in their segment. Then the story is passed to the next teller in the circle. They continue the story and incorporate their word or phrase, and so on until the end.

At the end of the story, the group can discuss the words. Was the word or phrase used correctly? Did it made sense in the story? Was it difficult to find a way to include your word or phrase? Did each storyteller set the next teller up well?

Variation: Have students pass their cards around so they receive a word or phrase at random to include in the story.

Helpful Hint: As in many storytelling and guessing games, the Leader may need to remind students that any contribution must "be in good taste."

Helpful Hint: To encourage players to include even more enriched vocabulary choices, have players guess which word was the word added from the index card. This will inspire students to use a number of unusual words as they tell their part of the story.

Story From a Picture

Goals addressed: Character Development, Cognitive Flexibility, Emotion Identification, Generating Alternatives, Improvisation Skills, Observation Skills, Problem-solving, Sequencing, Storytelling, Task Planning, Organization, Teamwork, Verbal Communication, etc.

Space requirements: Student can be at their desks.

Teacher/Counselor participation: Leader and Coach.

Numbers of students: Small teams of two to four.

Group version one: Collect photos, reproductions of paintings, or postcards that show interesting characters or activities. If the picturizations are rich with many possible ideas, have each group pick one and develop a story from it. They can write their story down and share it with the class. If students struggle with writing ideas down or have literacy issues, they can improvise a scene and act it out for the class. Then they can write their story down.

Group version two: If you have postcards of interesting characters, have each student pick a character that appeals to them. In a small group make up a story of what would happen if these characters came together. They can write down their story as a team or write out their version of the story individually. If they write their stories individually, they can read them to each other and compare the commonalities and differences.

If they are flexible enough, they might be able to combine their stories into one story (This will require flexibility and compromise because some ideas may need to be dropped or changed in order to fit with others). The group members can write out their jointly created story or act it out for the class. After performing the story, a script can be written from their scene.

Changing Perspectives (Dano Beal, 2014)

Goals Addressed: Character Development, Cognitive Empathy, Cognitive Flexibility, Critical Thinking, Decision-making, Generating Alternatives, Improvisational Skills, Problem-solving, Reframing, Perspective-taking, Sequencing, Task Planning, Organization, Teamwork, Verbal Communication, etc.

Space requirements: Acting/audience areas with space for rehearsal of several groups.

Teacher/Counselor participation: Leader and Coach.

Take a well-known story and have students re-write it from the perspective of a different character than the traditional protagonist or narrator. For instance, Little Red Riding Hood could be told from the perspective of the Wolf, the Grandmother, the Woodsman, or the Mother instead of Little Red. After they have been written, act out the stories.

If there are enough students, they could be divided into groups with the same number of characters as the chosen story, and each group could focus on creating the story from a different character's perspective. The stories could be acted out, and the class can discuss what happens when the perspective changes.

Glory Story (Jones, 1999)

Goals addressed: Accepting Praise Graciously, Character Development, Cognitive Empathy, Cognitive Flexibility, Decision-making, Generating Alternatives, Identifying What is Praiseworthy, Problem-solving, Sequencing, Social Connections, Storytelling, Task Planning and Organization, Teamwork, etc.

Space requirements: Work areas where small groups of students can create a story without being heard by the other groups.

Teacher/Counselor participation: Leader and Coach.

Supplies needed: Tables/desks, chairs, paper, and pencils.

Divide the class into small groups of two to six (depending on their abilities in working together). Assign each group to a different group. Each group will make up a story that involves all the members of their assigned group using the actual skills, strong points, or positive character traits of those individuals. The Leader circulates during the creation process to make sure all stories are appropriate, and no one is being turned into a scapegoat or being made fun of in the story. When the stories are done, each group reads their story or acts it out for the other groups.

Variation: Have each group write a story about themselves using their good points.

Typewriter (Belt & Stockley, 1989)

Goals addressed: Character Development, Cognitive Flexibility, Decision-making, Emotional Expression, Emotional Identification, Following Directions, Generating Alternatives, Improvisation Skills, Problem-solving, Sequencing, Shifting Emotions, Storytelling, Teamwork, and Verbal Communication.

Space requirements: Acting/Audience area.

Teacher/Counselor participation: Leader and Coach.

Number of Players: Two to five.

One player is the "Typist" (or Storyteller) and the other players are the actors in the story. The Typist asks the audience for a suggestion for the story: Either an object that must be in the story or a genre/style of story. The Typist sits at the side of the stage toward the back of the playing area so a good view can be had of the entire playing space. They face front so the audience can hear them clearly. The Typist can mime typing on a keyboard or writing in a journal, if they want to, or they can just focus on the stage.

The stage is bare at the beginning of the story, while the Typist sets the scene. Whenever a character is announced, he or she must enter. The actors improvise their actions and dialogue, but follow the narration provided by the Typist. The Typist creates a story with a beginning, middle, and end.

It is possible to "erase" characters, words, or actions. When the Typist says to erase an action or dialogue, the actors back up to where they were before that action was done or those words were said. Then they follow the directions of the Typist or, if improvising, try something new. If the Typist erases a character, that character has to leave the stage.

Helpful Hints: When students are learning this drama game, the Leader might want to be beside the Typist to side coach, if they get stuck or if they start being silly. If the Typist runs out of ideas, the Typist or Leader could take suggestions from the audience based on the story that has been created so far.

Cutting Room (Belt & Stockley, 1989)

Goals addressed: Character Development, Cognitive Flexibility, Decision-making, Emotional Expression, Emotional Identification, Following Directions, Generating Alternatives, Improvisation Skills, Problem-solving, Sequencing, Shifting Emotions, Storytelling, Teamwork, Tenses (Past-Present-Future), and Verbal Communication.

Space requirements: Acting/Audience area.

Teacher/Counselor participation: Leader and Coach.

This is an advanced version of Typewriter. The Narrator or "Film Editor" finds a place on the side of the performing area. The actors enter and begin to improvise a scene. Once the actors have created characters and the direction of the scene has begun to develop, the "Film Editor" can say, "Cut," the Actors freeze and listen as the Narrator provides a new time, place, and/or location for the actors to move to. In this version the actors have more control over the story, while the Narrator helps them structure the story by moving the scene forward or backwards at an appropriate time. (Time could move backward as in a flashback).

Puppet Shows

Goals addressed: Character Development, Cognitive Empathy, Cognitive Flexibility, Decision-making, Fine Motor Skills, Generating Alternatives, Inhibition, Initiation, Problem-solving, Sequencing, Storytelling, Task Initiation, Planning, Teamwork, Verbal Communication, etc.

Space requirements: Puppets and scripts could be created at students' desks. Performances will need a puppet stage-audience set up.

Teacher/Counselor participation: Leader, Coach, and Director.

Take a well-known story or a story being read in class and have students create a script for it. They could write it in small groups, or they could improvise it, record it, then write it down in script form (In a script only the dialogue and basic movements or sound effects are written down).

Cast each puppeteer as a character. Have puppeteers design on paper what their character looks like and then create a puppet from scratch. Practice the puppet show and present it for family and friends or for another class in school.

Helpful Hint: Sock puppets or wooden spoon puppets are relatively easy to make. Other materials that hold up well are paper plate puppets (use the thick Chinet plates rather than the thin plates. Glue them to tongue depressors for the necks of the characters). Another kind of sturdy puppet can be made from cardboard rolls of toilet paper or paper towels. They can also be glued to tongue depressors so puppeteers hands won't show. Paper bag puppets are not recommended because they tend to rip and show wear and tear easily.

Helpful Hint: Often, more than one student will want to be the same character. If so, there are a variety of ways to fairly divide up the parts:

- The Leader can cast the show, knowing who will be able to handle the bigger or more expressive parts.

- The names of all the characters can be put into a hat, and each student can pick one at random.

- Students could "audition" for several parts by creating voices for the character of their choice. The class can vote for who they think would do the best job.

Helpful Hint: To avoid having puppeteers memorize lines, the script can be written out and recorded. This provides practice with expressive reading. Puppeteers can practice their movements to the recording. Sometimes there is so much movement to remember backstage at a puppet show that also having to remember lines and speak loud enough to be heard by the audience can be difficult. Recording allows the puppeteers to concentrate on making their puppets expressive.

Helpful Hint: A long table with a tablecloth that reaches to the floor in the front or a short bookcase (approximately three-four feet tall) turned with its back to the audience can create simple puppet stages. Do not worry about creating a set. If you feel that a backdrop is necessary, fabric could be tacked to a bulletin board behind the stage or colored butcher paper could be taped to the wall. Don't try to change the scenery between scenes – have one backdrop that will work for the whole show.

Helpful Hint: Try to keep the number of puppeteers who are backstage for each show to no more than six, if possible. Puppetry requires a lot of moment, and puppeteers can end up getting into each other's space. The less puppeteers hiding out behind the stage, the fewer elbows, knees, and feet end up in other puppeteers' personal space.

 History

Famous Moments in History

Goals addressed: Bringing the Past to Life, Cognitive Empathy, Cognitive Flexibility, Emotion Identification, Generating Alternatives, Improvisation Skills, Problem-solving, Teamwork, and Verbal Communication.

Space required: Acting/audience areas.

Teacher/Counselor participation: Leader and Coach.

Choose an important historical moment that the class is studying. If there is a painting or illustration of the moment, use it as a guide to create a group sculpt of the moment. If there is no visual guide, create your own group sculpt.

Ask the actor playing each historical personage to share what they might be thinking and feeling at that moment. Do they realize this is an important occasion, or does it seem like any other day of the week? Discuss how they think this scene played out, then bring the scene to life.

Everyday Moments in History

Goals addressed: Bringing the Past to Life, Cognitive Empathy, Cognitive Flexibility, Emotion Identification, Generating Alternatives, Improvisation Skills, Perspective-taking, Problem-solving, Teamwork, and Verbal Communication.

Space required: Acting/audience areas.

Teacher/Leader participation: Leader and Coach.

Choose an historical period of time and a place (e.g., the Middle Ages in England, Ancient Egypt, Colonial America in Philadelphia) that the class is studying. Look at paintings or illustrations of how people dressed at the time, research what type of houses and occupations they had, what they ate and how they cooked, and other everyday aspects of life.

Create a group sculpt of how people with different statuses in society lived. The Leader can bring different characters to life and ask questions about their lives and points of view toward people at their level of society and those higher and lower than them. What are some the positive aspects of life at this time? What are some of the negative aspects?

If a particular set of relationships, class struggle, or set of customs catches the imagination of students, explore them more deeply through art, reproducing activities of the time, reading biographies, etc. Allow further research to guide them to an authentic reenactment of those customs or that struggle.

Famous People Come Alive

Goals addressed: Bringing the Past to Life, Cognitive Empathy, Critical Thinking, Decision-making, Generating Alternatives, Improvisation, Perspective-taking, Problem-solving, and Storytelling.

Space requirements: At first – students at their desks, later student in acting/audience spaces.

Teacher/Leader participation: Leader and Coach.

Ask students to decide on a person in history who they would like to learn more about. Have them read a book about the person's life. Coach them to find a moment of searching, of struggle, or of decision that person went through. Write a monologue from the point of view of that person. What were they thinking about? What were they feeling? Did they think they were going to succeed or fail? Why?

If you have access to costumes or fabric, each student could create a costume for their historical person. They could learn their monologue, practice presenting it with emotion and pacing, and present it in costume for a live performance. If students are nervous about performing or a good performance space is not available, their performances could be taped.

What Would Have Happened If …?

Goals addressed: Bringing the Past Alive, Cognitive Flexibility, Critical Thinking, Decision-making, Generating Alternatives, Perspective-taking, Problem-solving, and Storytelling.

Space requirements: Large open space.

Teacher/Counselor participation: Leader and Coach.

Leader preparation: Find a pivotal moment in the period of history that you are teaching.

Ask the students, "What would have happened if [the pivotal moment] did not happen?" For example, "What if the Confederacy had won the Civil War?" or "What could have happened if Marie Antoinette fed the starving people of France instead of saying, 'Let them eat cake.'" Brainstorm some of the possibilities and the results that could have happened.

At this point, a number of different activities could be done:

- Have each student write a story about what they think their life might have been like if one of the different possibilities had happened.

- Divide the class into smaller groups who want to explore one of the possibilities and give them time to brainstorm more ideas about the changes that might have occurred.

- Write a story about the change or create a short scene to express what might have happened.

 Geography

Singing Geography (Aycox, 1999).

Goals addressed: Breaking Words into Syllables, Listening skills, and Recognizing places/locations.

Space requirements: Students standing in a circle.

Teacher/Counselor participation: Leader and Coach.

One player leaves the room while the rest of the class decides on a place (country, city, state, etc.) and a well-known tune that is easy to sing (for example, "Home on the Range," "Pop Goes the Weasel," "Old MacDonald Had A Farm"). Break the name of the place into syllables. Each player in the circle chooses one of the syllables to sing. When the player returns to the room, the singing players start to sing the tune using their syllable instead of words. The player who had been gone must listen and has three guesses to put the syllables together into the name of the place.

Exploring the World

Goals addressed: Teamwork, Understanding Geographical and Spatial Relationships

Space requirements: Large open space.

Teacher/Counselor participation: Leader and Coach.

Supplies needed: Colored masking tape, maybe colored butcher paper cut into shapes.

In a large space, like a gymnasium or playground, create a map of your state, a country that you are studying, or the United States using masking tape on the floor or ground to designate boundaries. Rivers and lakes could be created with blue masking tape. Important cities could be created with a different color of masking tape. If you are using butcher paper shapes, use the colored masking tape to secure the paper on the floor/ground so no one slips.

Take students on a tour of the state or country, allowing them to walk a route from one place to another. Introduce state songs or national anthems, state birds, flowers, trees, etc., national symbols, flags, and unique geographical features. It will make a big difference to do this with students on their feet rather than sitting at their desks.

If you have students who have come from different parts of the world, create a world map and ask each student to stand on their country of origin. If you have students who have not grown up in your state, ask each one to stand on the state they were born in and then move to other states they have lived in. Finally, have everyone come home to your state. Students could also show each other what places they have visited on vacations or other trips.

Folk Dances From Different Countries

Goals addressed: Body Awareness, Body Control, Cognitive Flexibility, Following Directions, Gross Motor Skills, Rhythm, Sequencing, Social Connections, Spatial Awareness, Teamwork, Understanding a Different Culture through Movement and Music, and Working Memory.

Space requirements: An open space in which students can move.

Teacher/Counselor participation: Leader and Coach.

Supplies required: Recorded music to dance to or a musician who can play the music live. If you can find a video of the dance on the internet, it would help students understand the patterns and movements of the dance before learning on their own.

Teach the students a folk dance from one of the countries you are studying.

Songs From Different Countries

Goals addressed: Listening Skills, Rhythm, Teamwork, Understanding a Different Culture through their Music.

Space requirements: Students sitting at their desks.

Teacher/Counselor participation: Leader and Coach.

Supplies required: Recorded music of the song or a musician who can play the music live, Sheet music with the words. If you can find a video or recording of the song on the Internet, students can listen and will have an idea of the tune and pace of the song before they start learning it.

Stories From Different Cultures

Goals addressed: Cognitive Empathy, Emotion Identification, Improvisation Skills, Listening Skills, Perspective-taking, Sequencing, Storytelling, Understanding a Different Culture through its Folk Stories.

Space requirements: Students at their desks at first, then switch to an acting/audience area.

Teacher/Counselor participation: Storyteller and Coach.

Find a folktale from the culture you are studying that either clearly represents some aspect of that culture or is a version of a folktale we tell in our culture. Tell the story to the class and discuss what the story reveals about the culture. If it is a version of a story students know, discuss what is different and what that reveals about the culture you are studying as well as your own. Ask what the characters feel at different moments in the story. Have students pick their favorite scene from the story and act it out improvisationally.

 # Mathematics

Buzz

Goals addressed: Attention, Inhibition, Initiation, Multiples of numbers, Multiplication, Sequencing, Turn-taking, and Working Memory.

Space requirements: Students sitting in a circle.

Teacher/Counselor participation: Coach and Judge.

The Leader tells the players which number is "Buzz." One player begins counting from one and when a multiple of that number or a number that includes that number is reached, the player will say "Buzz," instead of the number.

For instance, if Buzz is five, counting would progress: one, two, three, four, BUZZ, six, seven, eight, nine, BUZZ, etc. If Buzz is seven, counting would progress: one, two, three, four, five, six, BUZZ, eight, nine, ten, eleven, twelve, thirteen, BUZZ, fifteen, sixteen, BUZZ, etc.

Variation: When it's time to say "Buzz," the player could be required to stand up and sit down again OR the players could be required to stand and remain standing until they said "Buzz" again. This version is good to use if students need to move in order to pay attention.

Amoeba

Goals addressed: Adding, Attention, Gross Motor Skills, Learning Numbers, Listening Skills, Social Connections, Spatial Awareness, Subtracting, and Teamwork.

Space requirements: Large open space where students can move.

Teacher/Counselor participation: Leader.

Players wander around the room in a random fashion. The Leader calls out a number, and the players get into a group of that number as quickly as possible. If they are missing a player or two, they can raise their fingers to show the number that they need, but they cannot shout the number out. If they end up with too many in their group, they have to get rid some players. If there is a "remainder" that is not large enough to create a group of the right size, those players are not "out." They can join in the next round.

As soon as the groups are created and checked, the group disperses and wanders around again until the next number is called.

Helpful Hint: Be sure that best friends are not walking together so that they end up in the same group each time. Players must walk in a random fashion and let chance create the groups.

Helpful Hint: Make sure players know that they may only eject someone from their group if they have more than the number called out *and* that if someone is ejected from a group because of "overpopulation," it is not a personal rejection. (Of course, the Leader needs to be aware of what is going on during the game. If someone keeps getting ejected again and again, that issue needs to be addressed appropriately.)

Variation: The Leader can change the size of the small groups by subtracting or adding players. The players have to figure out how to adjust. For instance, if there was a group of four, the Leader could say, "Plus two!" which would create new groups of six. However, instead of totally reforming groups, each group would try to get two new people to join it. Some groups might be divided between other groups while others just take on new members.

Putung Putung (Nelson & Glass, 1992)

Goals addressed: Attention, Listening Skills, Multiplication, Sequencing, and Working Memory.

Space requirements: Students sitting in a large circle.

Teacher/Counselor participation: Leader.

This is a Korean game which uses the Chinese word Putung (pooh-toong). Putung is the sound of a frog jumping into the water – what we might translate in English as "plop." If you would rather use "plop," please feel free to do so.

The first player in the circle starts by saying "One frog."

Second player says, "Two eyes."

Third player, "Four legs."

Fourth player, "Putung."

The fifth player starts over, but multiplies by two, "Two frogs."

Sixth player, "Four eyes."

Seventh player, "Eight legs."

Eight player, "Putung. Putung."

Ninth player, "Three frogs."

And so on.

The game can be played for a specified amount of time, and the group can see how many frogs they can create within that length of time. At a future playing of the game, the class can see if they can beat their previous record and send more frogs into the pond.

Twenty-one (Jones, 1999)

Goals addressed: Addition, Attention, Teamwork, and Working Memory.

Space requirements: Circle with students standing.

Teacher/Counselor participation: Leader and Coach.

Numbers of students: Teams of three to nine members.

Rule One for this game is that it must be played with no talking!

Previous to starting the game, the Leader decides how many rounds will be played or how much time will be spent playing the game. Each team has one person who volunteers to be the Counter for that round. The other players put both hands behind their backs. The Leader says, "One, two, three," and on "three" all the players bring their hands into the circle and show between one and ten fingers on their hands, freezing in that position. The Counter in each circle counts all the fingers and if the circle has 21 fingers showing, they "win" the round. This means that more than one circle can "win" during one round. Players MAY NOT change the number of fingers they have shown once they have displayed their hands!

For the next round, a different player becomes the Counter. No talking can happen among each circle to arrange a strategy. That would be cheating. The circle must get to 21 by chance.

At the end of the time allotted for the game or the number of rounds predetermined, discuss which circle was the most successful at reaching 21, and why they thought they were able to achieve it so often. Were they working together? Did they find a way to communicate with each other?

Survival Shopping (Jones, 1999)

Goals addressed: Addition, Budgeting, Cognitive Empathy, Cognitive Flexibility, Critical Thinking, Decision-making. Generating Alternatives, Inhibition, Listening Skills, Perspective-taking, Problem-solving, Teamwork, Verbal Communication, and Working Memory.

Space requirements: A workspace big enough for a small group.

Teacher/Counselor participation: Leader and Coach.

Divide the class into teams of two to six players. Give each group a catalogue or a website from a sports equipment store, toy store, clothing store, department store, or gift store. They have $200 (or another amount that makes sense for the size of the group and what they have to buy) to spend. Their task is to buy gifts for the players in another group for a special birthday celebration. They have to figure out what each student in the other group might like and what they could buy so that each one in that group has a present they would really enjoy, but money spent on the gifts doesn't go over budget.

Variation: Players have a budget and a gift catalogue or specific website and must decide how they will find the perfect gift for their mothers for Mother's Day, spending approximately the same range of money on each mother.

After students share their purchases and show that they stayed within their budgets, ask them how they each decided what their mother would like as a gift? How did they come to agreement on how to divide the money? Did they work well together, or could they have done better?

Variation: Players will be taking a trip to Mars, and it will take one year to get there. They must buy everything that they will need on the journey (or you could give them a list of items they need to get for the journey). They cannot go over the budgeted amount, and they must use the catalogues or websites you have given them.

Variation: Players will be taking a trip to the West in a covered wagon and must make sure they have all the food, clothing, and tools they will need to create a new homestead.

After students share their equipment list, ask how they decided what they needed and how they came to their agreement. Did they work well together, or could they have done better?

Elastablasts (Also Called Cooperabands And Buddy Bands)

Goals addressed: Body Awareness, Body Control, Geometry/Shapes, Gross Motor Skills, Sensory Integration and Awareness, Spatial Awareness, Task Planning-Organization, Teamwork, etc.

Space requirements: Large open space.

Teacher/Counselor participation: Player and Coach.

Supplies needed: At least one large Elastablast Exercise Band (24 feet in diameter for 10–20 people), Long tape measure, Small individual elastic stretch bands.

Elastablasts are large bungee cords covered in soft, colorful fleece material. They are fun to play with and easy to hold onto. They create a connection among all members of a group because when one player pulls on the band, it effects everyone else holding on.

For the purposes of geometry, use large elastablasts to explore making different shapes: circles, ovals, squares, rectangles, triangles, polygons, five point stars, six point stars, etc.

Using the tape measure, find the area of different shapes using the appropriate formula.

Have students use the smaller individual stretch bands to create different shapes on their own. By creating shapes with each other and by themselves, they develop a clear understanding of the differences between shapes.

Conclusion

The ideas in this chapter just scratch the surface of embodied learning experiences that can be brought into your classroom. Having used the games in this book that improve executive functions, you now understand which practices are engaging for your students and which positively grow their organization and focusing abilities. You will be able to identify other games that do the same type of skill building to provide variety or additional practice in certain areas. You will most likely be able to start inventing your own drama games and explorations.

I am sometimes told that including active learning in the public school curriculum takes up a lot of time that instead needs to be spent on review, practice, and other aspects of the curriculum. However, capturing students' attention, generating their curiosity, and immersing them deeply in experiences that are memorable, pays off. Embodied learning often incorporates information across disciplines and increases students' problem-solving abilities, critical thinking skills, and decision-making. Wider and deeper thinking will allow your students to succeed on standardized tests, even if you have not spent time teaching to the test.

Teaching your students improvisation has allowed you to learn improvisational skills yourself. It is quite possible that you have started to feel more comfortable and creative in your work, and you feel less hesitant allowing your students up out of their seats to work on projects and interact. Saying "Yes, and …" opens options to break old habits and bring more excitement and joy into the classroom.

References

Aycox, F. (1999). *Games we should play in school, 2nd ed*. Front Row Experience.

Beal, D. (2014, March 29) *Games for the classroom* {Conference session]. Theatre in Our Schools, American Alliance of Theatre in Education, Seattle, WA, United States.

Belt, L., & Stockley, R. (1989). *Improvisation through theatre sports*. Thespis Productions.

Fugate, J. M. B., Macrine, S. L., & Cipriano, C. (2019). The role of embodied cognition for transforming learning. *International Journal of School & Educational Psychology*, 7(4), 274–288.

Jones, A. (1999). *Team-building activities for every group*. Rec Room Publishing.

Nelson, W. E., & Glass, H. B. (1992). *International playtime: Classroom games and dances from around the world*. Frank Schaffer Publications, Inc.

Sawyer, K. (2019). *The creative classroom: Innovative teaching for 21st-century learners*. Teachers College Press.

Shapiro, L., & Stolz, S. A. (2019). Embodied cognition and its significance for education. *Theory and Research in Education*, 17(1), 19–39.

Appendix

Drama Games, Improvisations, and Activities Organized by Executive Functions, Social-Emotional Skills, and Academic Subjects.

Executive Functions

Metacognition

Attention

1776
ABC through Z
Add on Memory Games
Amoeba
Backwriting
Buzz
Chain Pantomime
Change Three
Conflict-Cooperation Drawings
Civil Disobedience
Conversation Practice
Counting 1–20
Drumming/Percussion Conversation
Dude!
Elephant and Giraffe
Finding Spaces
Follow the Leader

Fortunately-Unfortunately
Giving/Taking Directions to Build a
  Design
Go
Go Around Pantomimes
Group Drawing
Group Storytelling
I'm Thinking of a Word That
  Rhymes with …
In Plain View
Jerusalem/Jericho
Listening to Drums (Rhythmic
  Conversations)
Magic Dollar Bill Trick
Magic Scarf
Magic Stick/Magic Tube
Magical Power

Mirroring
Museum Guard/Night at the Museum
Name Game: Pass Your Name and
    a Movement Around the Circle
Pantomime Down the Line
Partner Pantomimes
Pass the Sound/Pass the Movement
Pattern Ball Passing
People – Shelter – Storm
Putang Putang
Sarvisilla
Scene with Three Props
Shape Copying
Simon Says
Sushi
Telephone
Three Ball Pass
Twenty-One
Who's the Leader?
Yes-No-You
Zip-Zap-Zop

Attention Shifting

1776
Elephant and Giraffe
Go
Introductions
On the Bank/In the River
Pass the Sound/Pass the Movement
People-Shelter-Storm
Sushi
Three Ball Pass
Yes-No-You
Zip-Zap-Zop

Observation Skills

Chain Pantomime

Change Three
Chosen
I'm Thinking of a Word That
    Rhymes with …
In Plain View
In the Manner of the Word
Magic Scarf
Magic Stick/Magic Tube
Mirroring
Observing Emotions on Video
Observing Escalation and
    De-Escalation of Emotions
    on Video
Pantomime Down the Line
Partner Pantomimes
Shape Copying
Story from a Picture
Terrible Magician
Who's the Leader?

Self-Reflection/Self-Awareness

Categories in Order
Decisions, Decisions!
Four Corners
Haiku Activities
Locograms/Categorial
    Groupings
Saying "No, thanks" to Thrill-
    Seeking Behavior
Sculpts and Scenes Involved in a
    Bullying Situation
Self-Advocacy: Explaining
    Accommodations Needed
    for School or a Job
Spectrograms
Telling the Truth When Under
    Pressure to Lie

Sequencing

ABC through Z

Alphabet Race

Add on Memory Games

Animal Dance

Backwriting

Body-Spelling

Buzz

Categories in Order

Chain Pantomime

Count 1–20

Cutting Room

Folk Dances from Different Countries

Fortunately-Unfortunately

Giving/Taking Directions to Build a
  Design

Glory Story

Going to a Restaurant

Group Storytelling

Hand Squeezes/Pass the Pulse

Introductions

Labor Dance

Machines

Magic Dollar Bill Trick

Making a Phone Call to a Friend to
  Plan an Outing

Ordering Fast Food Delivery

Pantomime Down the Line

Pattern Ball Passing

People-Shelter-Storm

Puppet Shows

Putang Putang

Spectrograms

Stories from Different Cultures

Story from a Picture

Typewriter

Yes, and … Storytelling

Yes-No-You

Zip-Zap-Zop

Working Memory

1776

Add on Memory Games

Animal Dance

Buzz

Chain Pantomime

Change Three

Chosen

Folk Dances from Different
  Countries

Fortunately-Unfortunately

Go

Group Storytelling

Labor Dance

Magic Dollar Bill Trick

Magic Scarf

Magic Stick/Magic Tube

Making a Phone Call to a Friend
  to Plan an Outing

Name Game: Pass Your Name and
  a Movement Around the Circle

Ordering Fast Food Delivery

Pantomime Down the Line

Partner Pantomimes

Pattern Ball Passing

People-Shelter-Storm

Putang Putang

Scene with Three Props

Shape Copying

Survival Shopping

Sushi

Telephone

The Captain is Coming

Three Ball Pass

Twenty-One
Yes, and … Storytelling

Emotional Regulation

Conflict-Cooperation Drawings
Emotion Targets
Going to a Restaurant
Group Drawing
Saying "No, thanks" to Thrill-
    Seeking Behavior
Sculpting Conflict
Scenes of Escalation and
    De-Escalation
Self-Advocacy: Explaining
    Accommodations Needed
    for School or a Job
Telling the Truth When Under
    Pressure to Lie

Cognitive Empathy

Changing Perspectives
Cutting Room
Emotion Map
Emotion Spectrogram
Emotional Orchestra/Symphony
    with Sounds
Emotional Orchestra/Symphony
    with Words
Everyday Moments in History
Failure Celebration
Failure Inoculation
Famous Moments in History
Famous People Come Alive
Glory Story
Group Mood
Making an Entrance

Observing Emotions on Video
Observing Escalation and
    De-Escalation of Emotions on Video
Puppet Shows
Saying "No, thanks" to Thrill-
    Seeking Behavior
Sculpting Conflict
Sculpting Emotions
Sculpts and Scenes Involved in a
    Bullying Situation
Stories from Different Countries
Survival Shopping
Telling the Truth When Under
    Pressure to Lie
Terrible Magician
Typewriter
Yes, and …
Yes, and … Scenes
Yes, and … Storytelling

Emotion Identification

Cutting Room
Emotion Map
Emotion Spectrogram
Emotion Walks
Emotional Greetings
Emotional Orchestra/Symphony
    with Sounds
Emotional Orchestra/Symphony
    with Words
Everyday Moments in History
Famous Moments in History
Group Mood
Making an Entrance
Observing Emotions on Video
Observing Escalation and De-
    Escalation of Emotions on Video

Pass the Face
Pass the Face Reactions
Sculpting Conflict
Sculpting Emotions
Stories from Different Cultures
Story from a Picture
Typewriter

Emotion Intensity Identification

Emotion Spectrogram
Emotional Orchestra/Symphony
with Sounds
Emotional Orchestra/Symphony
with Words
Group Mood
Making an Entrance
Observing Emotions on Video
Pass the Face
Pass the Face Reactions
Sculpting Conflict
Sculpting Emotions

Emotional Empathy

Any Kind of Sculpting for the "Clay"
Conflict-Cooperation Drawings
Pass the Face Reactions
Yes, and …

Emotional Expression

Cutting Room
Emotion Spectrogram
Emotion Targets
Emotion Walks
Emotional Greetings
Emotional Orchestra/Symphony
with Sounds

Emotional Orchestra/Symphony
with Words
Group Mood
Making an Entrance
Pass the Face
Pass the Face Reactions
Sculpting Conflict
Sculpting Emotions
Sculpts and Scenes Involved in
a Bullying Situation
It's Tuesday!
Typewriter

Emotional Tolerance

Failure Celebration
Failure Vaccination
Terrible Magician

Shifting Emotions

Cutting Room
Deep Breathing
Emotion Map
Emotion Targets
Grounding
Observing Escalation and
De-Escalation of Emotions on
Video
Scenes of Escalation and De-Escalation
Typewriter

Stress Management, Relaxation, and Emotional Release

Diaphragmatic Breathing
Emotion Targets
Four Part Breath
Failure Celebration
Failure Vaccination

Grounding
Pressure Nouns
Progressive Relaxation
Scenes of Escalation and
    De-Escalation
Terrible Magician

Behavioral Regulation

Conflict-Cooperation Drawings
Emotion Targets
Going to a Restaurant
Group Drawing
I'm Thinking of a Word That Rhymes
    with …
Job Interview
Observing Escalation and
    De-Escalation of Emotions on
    Video
Sculpting Conflict
Sculpts of the Characters Involved
    in a Bullying Situation
Scenes of Escalation and
    De-Escalation
Saying "No, thanks" to
    Thrill-Seeking Behavior
Self-Advocacy: Explaining
    Accommodations Needed for
    School or a Job
Telling the Truth When Under
    Pressure to Lie

Body Awareness

Come-Go-Stay
Elastablasts
Folk Dances from Different
    Countries

Hula Hoop/Bubble Walk
Personal Space
Sculpting Conflict
Sculpting Emotions

Body Control

Animal Transformations
Body-Spelling
Civil Disobedience
Dog and Bone
Elastablasts
Emotion Walks
Environmental Walks
Finding Spaces
Find Your Partner with a Sound
Folk Dancing from Different
    Countries
Follow the Leader
Freeze
Heads, Shoulders, Knees, and
    Toes
Hot Chocolate River
Labor Dance/Animal Dance
Machines
Magical Power
Mirroring
Museum Guard/Night at the
    Museum
On the Bank/In the River
Pass the Sound/Pass the
    Movement
Relay Race with No Hands
Shape Copying
Shoe Walks
Simon Says
The Queen/King has a Headache
Yes-No-You

Boundaries

Body Boundaries/Personal Space
Come-Go-Stay
Finding Spaces
Follow the Leader
Go
Hand Squeezes/Pass the Pulse
Machines
Magical Power
On the Bank/In the River
Relay Race with No Hands

Cognitive Flexibility

Add on Memory Games
Changing Perspectives
Conflict-Cooperation Drawings
Conversation Practice
Corridors I
Corridors II
Cutting Room
Drumming/Percussion
    Conversation
Everyday Moments in History
Failure Celebration
Failure Inoculation
Famous Moments in History
Folk Dances from Different
    Countries
Fortunately-Unfortunately
Glory Story
Group Drawing
Group Storytelling
Magic Scarf
Magic Stick/Magic Tube
Name Game: Pass Your Name and
    a Movement Around the Circle
Partner Pantomimes

Puppet Shows
Scenes of Escalation and
    De-Escalation
Secret Agenda
Story from a Picture
Survival Shopping
Terrible Magician
The Snail
Typewriter
What Would Have Happened
    If …?
Yes, and …
Yes, and … Scenes
Yes, and … Storytelling

Decision Making

Appropriate or Inappropriate?
Categories in Order
Changing Perspectives
Come-Go-Stay
Cutting Room
Decisions, Decisions!
Famous Moments in History
Famous People Come Alive
Fortunately-Unfortunately
Four Corners
Giving/Taking Directions to Build
    a Design
Glory Story
Going to a Restaurant
Group Storytelling
Job Interviews
Locograms/Categorical Groupings
Magic Scarf
Magic Stick/Magic Tube
Partner Pantomimes
Puppet Shows

Saying "No, thanks" to Thrill-
Seeking Behavior
Scene with Three Props
Scenes of Escalation and
De-Escalation
Sculpting Conflict
Self-Advocacy: Explaining
Accommodations Needed
for School or a Job
Spectrograms
Survival Shopping
Telling the Truth When Under
Pressure to Lie
The Snail
Typewriter
What Would Have Happened
If …?
Yes, and …
Yes, and … Scenes
Yes, and … Storytelling

Fine Motor Skills

Giving/Taking Directions to Build a
Design
Magic Dollar Bill Trick
Puppet Shows

Following Directions

Come-Go-Stay
Cutting Room
Folk Dances in Different Countries
Giving/Taking Directions to Build a
Design
Go
People-Shelter-Storm
Simon Says

Sushi
The Captain is Coming
Typewriter

Generating Alternatives

Changing Perspectives
Cutting Room
Everyday Moments in History
Famous Moments in History
Fortunately-Unfortunately
Famous People Come Alive
Glory Story
Group Storytelling
Hot Chocolate River
I'm Thinking of a Word That Rhymes
with …
Machines
Magic Scarf
Magic Stick/Magic Tube
Partner Pantomimes
Pressure Nouns
Puppet Shows
Relay Race with No Hands
Saying "No, thanks" to Thrill-
Seeking Behavior
Scene with Three Props
Sculpting Conflict
Story from a Picture
Survival Shopping
Telling the Truth When Under
Pressure to Lie
The Snail
Typewriter
What Would Have Happened If …?
Yes, and …
Yes, and … Scenes
Yes, and … Storytelling

Gross Motor Skills

Amoeba
Animal Dance
Animal Transformations
Body-Spelling
Elastablasts
Folk Dancing from Different
    Countries
Heads, Shoulders, Knees, and
    Toes
I'm Thinking of a Word That
    Rhymes with …
In the Manner of the Word
Labor Dance
Machines
Museum Guard/Night at the
    Museum
Relay Race with No Hands
Shoe Walks
Simon Says

Inhibition/Impulse Control

ABC through Z
Animal Transformations
Appropriate or Inappropriate?
Buzz
Civil Disobedience
Counting 1–20
Dog and Bone
Emotion Walks
Emotional Orchestra/Symphony
Emotional Orchestra/Symphony
    with Words
Environmental Walks
Freeze
Go
Heads, Shoulders, Knees, and Toes

I'm Thinking of a Word That
    Rhymes with …
Jerusalem/Jericho
Museum Guard/Night at the
    Museum
On the Bank/In the River
Puppet Shows
Sarvisilla
Scenes of Escalation and
    De-Escalation
Shoe Walks
Simon Says
Survival Shopping
The Queen/King Has a Headache
Yes, and …
Yes, and … Scenes
Yes, and … Storytelling

Initiation

ABC through Z
Buzz
Civil Disobedience
Corridors I
Corridors II
Counting 1–20
Dude!
Go
Going to a Restaurant
Group Drawing
Heads, Shoulders, Knees, and Toes
Introductions
Job Interviews
Machines
Making a Phone Call to a
    Friend to Plan an Outing
Museum Guard/Night at the Museum
Ordering Fast Food Delivery

Partner Pantomimes
Puppet Shows
Scenes of Escalation and
    De-Escalation
Sculpts and Scenes Involved in
    Bullying Situations
Self-Advocacy: Explaining
    Accommodations Needed for
    School or a Job
Yes, and …
Yes, and … Scenes
Yes, and … Storytelling

Opposite Actions

Appropriate or Inappropriate?
Civil Disobedience
Failure Celebration
Failure Vaccination
Go
Heads, Shoulders, Knees, and Toes
    Reversal

Problem Solving

Changing Perspectives
Chosen
Corridors I
Corridors II
Cutting Room
Everyday Moments in History
Famous Moments in History
Famous People Come Alive
Fortunately-Unfortunately
Glory Story
Group Storytelling
Hot Chocolate River
Magic Scarf

Magic Stick/Magic Tube
Making a Phone Call to a Friend
    to Plan an Outing
Museum Guard/Night at the
    Museum
Partner Pantomimes
Puppet Show
Relay Race with No Hands
Saying "No, thanks" to Thrill-
    Seeking Behavior
Scene with Three Props
Scenes of Escalation and
    De-Escalation
Sculpting Conflict
Self-Advocacy: Explaining
    Accommodations Needed for
    School or a Job
Story from a Picture
Survival Shopping
Telling the Truth When Under
    Pressure to Lie
Terrible Magician
The Snail
Typewriter
What Would Have Happened
    If …?
Who's the Leader?
Yes, and …
Yes, and … Scenes
Yes… and… Storytelling

Reframing

Changing Perspectives
Failure Celebration
Failure Inoculation
Fortunately-Unfortunately
Terrible Magician

Rhythm

Animal Dance
Changing Perspectives
Elastablasts
Emotion Map
Famous People Come Alive
Folk Dances in Different Countries
Giving/Taking Directions to Build a
   Design
Glory Story
Haiku Activities
Hot Chocolate River
Labor Dance
Listening with Drums (Rhythm
   Conversation)
Making a Phone Call to a Friend to
   Plan an Outing
Ordering Fast Food Delivery
Pattern Ball Passing
Puppet Show
Relay Race with No Hands
Scene with Three Props
Self-Advocacy: Explaining
   Accommodations Needed
   for School or a Job
Songs from Different Countries
Story from a Picture
Task Planning, Organization,
   Initiation, Evaluation, etc.

Teamwork

1776
ABC through Z
Alphabet Race
Amoeba
Animal Dance

Backwriting
Body-Spelling
Changing Perspectives
Come-Go-Stay
Corridors I
Corridors II
Counting 1-20
Cutting Room
Dog and Bone
Elastablasts
Elephant and Giraffe
Emotional Orchestra/Symphony
   with Sounds
Emotional Orchestra/Symphony
   with Words
Environments
Everyday Moments in History
Exploring the World
Famous Moments in History
Folk Dances from Different
   Countries
Follow the Leader
Fortunately-Unfortunately
Giving/Taking Directions to Build a
   Design
Glory Story
Group Drawings
Hot Chocolate River
I'm Thinking of a Word That
   Rhymes with …
Labor Dance
Machines
Magical Power
Mirroring
Museum Guard/Night at the
   Museum
Parachutes
Partner Pantomimes

Pass the Sound/Pass the
    Movement
Pattern Ball Passing
People-Shelter-Storm
Puppet Show
Relay Race with No Hands
Scarf Ball Toss
Scene with Three Props
Scenes of Escalation and
    De-Escalation
Sculpting Conflict
Sculpting Emotions
Songs from Different Countries
Story from a Picture
Survival Shopping
Terrible Magician
The Captain is Coming
The Queen/King has a
    Headache
Twenty-One
Typewriter
Who's the Leader?
Yes, and …

Yes, and … Scenes
Yes, and … Storytelling

Turn Taking

ABC through Z
Backwriting
Buzz
Conflict-Cooperation Drawing
Corridors I
Corridors II
Counting 1–20
Go Around Pantomimes
Group Drawing
Group Storytelling
I'm Thinking of a Word That
    Rhymes with …
In the Manner of the Word
Magic Scarf
Magic Stick/Magic Tube
Partner Pantomimes
Sculpting Conflict
Secret Agenda

Sensory Integration Issues

Sensory Integration and Awareness

Backwriting
Dog and Bone
Elastablasts
Find Your Partner with a Sound
Hand Squeezes/Pass the Pulse
Mirroring
Pass the Sound/Pass the Movement
Santa's Elves

The Queen/King has a Headache
Who's the Leader?

Spatial Awareness

Amoeba
Elastablasts

Finding Spaces
Find Your Partner with a Sound
Folk Music from Different
   Countries

Hula Hoop/Bubble Walk
Night at the Museum/Night
   Guard
The Captain is Coming

 # Social-Emotional Skills

Social Skills

Accepting Encouragement

Failure Celebration
Failure Inoculation
Greeting Cards
Manito
Terrible Magician

Go
Introductions
Mirroring
Yes-No-You
Zip-Zap-Zop

Accepting Praise Graciously

Circle of Acknowledgement
Circle of Appreciation
Glory Story
Manito
Notes of Acknowledgment
Superhero Capes

Identifying What is Praiseworthy

Circle of Acknowledgment
Circle of Appreciation
Glory Story
Manito
Superhero Capes

Personal Space

Body Boundaries/Personal Space
Come-Go-Stay
Finding Spaces
Hula Hoop/Bubble Walk

Encouraging Another

Circle of Acknowledgment
Circle of Appreciation
Greeting Cards
Superhero Capes

Perspective Taking

Changing Perspectives
Cutting Room
Everyday Moments in History

Eye Contact

Come-Go-Stay
Dude!

Famous Moments in History
Glory Story
Puppet Show
Stories from Different Cultures
Survival Shopping
Typewriter
What Would Have Happened If …?

Social Connection

Amoeba
Folk Dancing from Different
    Countries
Glory Story
Introductions
Locograms
Mirroring
Partner Pantomimes
Spectrograms
Yes-No-You
Zip-Zap-Zop

Social Skills

Appropriate or Inappropriate?
Going to a Restaurant
Introductions
Job Interviews
Making a Phone Call to a Friend
    to Plan an Outing
Museum Guard/Night at the Museum
Ordering Fast Food Delivery
Saying "No, thanks" to Thrill-
    Seeking Behavior
The Snail
Telling the Truth When Under
    Pressure to Lie
Yes, and …
Yes, and … Scenes

Yes, and … Storytelling

Working Under Pressure

Cutting Room
Pressure Nouns
Puppet Show
Typewriter

Communication Skills

Listening Skills

Amoeba
Animal Transformations
Conversation Practice
Corridors I
Corridors II
Counting 1–20
Dog and Bone
Drumming/Percussion
    Conversation
Environmental Walks
Find Your Partner with a Sound
Fortunately-Unfortunately
Freeze
Giving/Taking Directions to Build a
    Design
Going to a Restaurant
Group Storytelling
Heads, Shoulders, Knees, and Toes
Jerusalem/Jericho
Job Interviews
Listening with Drums (Rhythm
    Conversation)
Making a Phone Call to a Friend to
    Plan an Outing
On the Bank/In the River
Ordering Fast Food Delivery

People-Shelter-Storm

Putang Putang

Santa's Elves

Sarvisilla

Scenes of Escalation and
    De-Escalation

Secret Agenda

Self-Advocacy: Explaining
    Accommodations Needed
    for School or a Job

Shoe Walks

Simon Says

Singing Geography

Songs from Different Countries

Stories from Different Cultures

Survival Shopping

Sushi

Telephone

The Captain is Coming

The Snail

The Queen/King Has a Headache

Tone of Voice Practice – One Word
    Scenes

Yes, and…

Yes, and … Scenes

Yes, and … Storytelling

Non-Verbal Communication

ABC through Z

Come-Go-Stay

Conflict-Cooperation Drawings

Counting 1–20

Drumming/Percussion
    Conversation

Dude!

Emotion Walks

Emotional Greetings

Environments

Group Drawings

Group Mood

Go Around Pantomimes

I'm Thinking of a Word That
    Rhymes with …

It's Tuesday!

In the Manner of the Word

Job Interviews

Listening with Drums (Rhythm
    Conversation)

Magic Scarf

Magic Stick/Magic Tube

Making an Entrance

Mirroring

Museum Guard/Night at the
    Museum

Partner Pantomimes

Pass the Face

Pass the Face Reactions

Scene with Three Props

Sculpting Conflict

Sculpting Emotions

Sculpts and Scenes Involved in a
    Bullying Situation

Self-Advocacy: Explaining
    Accommodations Needed for
    School or a Job

Tone of Voice Practice – One Word
    Dialogues

Verbal Communication

Appropriate or Inappropriate?

Changing Perspectives

Cutting Room

Dude!

Emotional Greetings

Everyday Moments in History
Famous Moments in History
Famous People Come Alive
Fortunately-Unfortunately
Going to a Restaurant
Glory Story
Group Storytelling
Haiku Activities
It's Tuesday!
Job Interviews
Making a Phone Call to a Friend to Plan an Outing
Ordering Fast Food Delivery
Puppet Show
Saying "No, thanks" to Thrill-Seeking Behavior
Scene with Three Props

Scenes of Escalation and De-Escalation
Sculpts and Scenes Involved in Bullying Situations
Secret Agenda
Self-Advocacy: Explaining Accommodations Needed for School or a Job
Story from a Picture
Survival Shopping
Telling the Truth When Under Pressure to Lie
The Snail
Tone of Voice Practice – One Word Dialogues
Typewriter

Improvisation Skills

Appropriate or Inappropriate?
Changing Perspectives
Conflict-Cooperation Drawings
Corridors I
Corridors II
Cutting Room
Environments
Everyday Moments in History
Failure Celebration
Failure Inoculation
Famous Moments in History
Famous People Come Alive
Going to a Restaurant
Group Drawing
I'm Thinking of a Word That Rhymes with …
In the Manner of the Word

Introductions
It's Tuesday!
Job Interviews
Making a Phone Call to a Friend to Plan an Outing
Museum Guard/Night at the Museum
Ordering Fast Food Delivery
Puppet Show
Saying "No, thanks" to Thrill-Seeking Behavior
Scene with Three Props
Scenes of Escalation and De-Escalation
Sculpting Conflict II
Sculpts and Scenes Involved in Bullying Situations

Self-Advocacy: Explaining
  Accommodations Needed for
  School or a Job
Story from a Picture
Stories from Different Cultures
Telling the Truth When Under
  Pressure to Lie

Terrible Magician
The Snail
Typewriter
What Would Have Happened If …?
Yes., and …
Yes, and … Scenes
Yes, and … Storytelling

 # Academic Skills and Curricular Subjects

Critical Thinking

Changing Perspectives
Decisions, Decisions!
Discussions
Famous Moments in History
Famous People Come Alive
Four Corners
Locograms/Categorical Groupings
Saying "No, thanks" to Thrill-
  Seeking Behavior
Secret Agenda
Spectrograms
Sculpting Conflict
Sculpts and Scenes Involved in a
  Bullying Situation
Survival Shopping
Telling the Truth When Under
  Pressure to Lie
What Would Have Happened If …?

Singing Geography
Songs from Different Countries
Stories from Different Cultures

History

Everyday Moments in History
Famous People Come Alive
Famous Moments in History
What Would Have Happened
  If?

Language Arts

Character Development

Changing Perspectives
Cutting Room
Famous Moments in
  History
Glory Story
Puppet Show
Story from a Picture
Typewriter

Geography and Other Cultures

Exploring the World
Folk Dances from Different Countries

Letter Recognition

Alphabet Race
Body Spelling

Identifying Parts of Speech

In the Manner of the Word
Pressure Nouns

Identifying Syllables

Haiku Activities
Singing Geography

Rhyme

I'm Thinking of a Word That
    Rhymes with …

Spelling

Alphabet Race
Body Spelling

Storytelling-Storywriting

Changing Perspectives
Cutting Room
Famous Moments in History
Famous People Come Alive
Fortunately-Unfortunately

Glory Story
Group Storytelling
Puppet Show
Secret Agenda
Story from a Picture
Stories from Different Cultures
Typewriter
What Would Have Happened If …?
Yes, and … Storytelling

Vocabulary Enhancement

Secret Agenda

Verb Tenses

Cutting Room

Writing

Thank You Note for a Job Interview

Mathematics

Amoeba
Buzz
Elastablasts for Geometry
Putung Putung
Survival Shopping
Twenty-One

Index of Games, Improvisations, Activities, Figures, and Table

Printed in the United States
by Baker & Taylor Publisher Services